Scott Foresman

Grade 3
Unit and End-of-Year
Benchmark Tests
Teacher's Manual

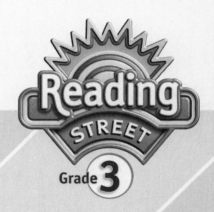

Reading STREET
Grade 3

PEARSON

Glenview, Illinois • Boston, Massachusetts • Chandler, Arizona • Upper Saddle River, New Jersey

The Pearson Promise

As the largest educational publishing company in the world, Pearson is committed to providing you with curriculum that not only meets the Common Core State Standards, but also supports your implementation of these standards with your students.

Pearson has aligned the Common Core State Standards to every grade level of *Scott Foresman Reading Street,* our premier educational curriculum. This product provides an alignment of the Common Core State Standards to the Grade 3 assessment items in *Scott Foresman Reading Street Unit and End-of-Year Benchmark Tests.*

We value your partnership highly and look forward to continuing our mission to provide educational materials that fully satisfy your classroom needs.

ISBN-13: 978-0-328-68393-2
ISBN-10:   0-328-68393-0
9 10 V001 15 14

Contents

Overview **T5**

Administering the Tests **T6**

Scoring the Tests **T10**

Interpreting Test Results **T20**

Evaluation Charts **T31**

Class Record Chart **T45**

Answer Keys **T47**

Optional — Fluency Checks or Running Records **T57**

Benchmark Tests **1**

    Unit 1

    Unit 2

    Unit 3

    Unit 4

    Unit 5

    Unit 6

    End-of-Year

OVERVIEW

Scott Foresman *Reading Street* provides a wide array of formal tests and classroom assessments to support instruction. Formal assessments include the following:

- Baseline Group Tests

- Weekly Selection Tests

- Fresh Reads for Differentiated Test Practice

- Unit and End-of-Year Benchmark Tests aligned to Common Core State Standards

This Teacher's Manual provides information for administering the Benchmark Tests, scoring the tests, and interpreting the results. Detailed information about other assessment materials and procedures may be found in the *Assessment Handbook*.

Description of the Benchmark Tests

In Grade 3, there are six Unit Benchmark Tests—one for each unit—and an End-of-Year Benchmark Test. The Unit Benchmark Tests are designed to measure student progress based on the comprehension skills and strategies, literary elements, vocabulary, phonics skills, writing conventions, and types of writing taught in each unit. The End-of-Year Benchmark Test measures skills covered in all six units. The Benchmark Tests offer an integrated approach to assessment by measuring all skills and strategies in relation to reading selections.

In addition, the Benchmark Tests are designed to provide practice in test-taking skills and to prepare students to take the Reading/Language Arts section of standardized tests, state tests, or teacher-made tests. The tests include both multiple-choice and constructed-response questions. They also include writing prompts that will help students prepare for state writing tests.

Each Unit Benchmark Test has these features:

- Each test has two components—Reading – Parts 1–4 and Writing – Part 5.

- Reading – Part 1 presents two selections in different genres. The genres of these selections, drawn from fiction and nonfiction, reflect genres taught in each unit.

- Each selection reflects the theme of the unit.

- Reading – Parts 1–4 contain forty multiple-choice questions and two constructed-response questions. These questions test reading comprehension, literary elements, critical thinking skills, vocabulary strategies, phonics skills, and writing conventions. Some of the items measure the ability to synthesize information and to compare and contrast across texts.

- Writing – Part 5 of each test presents a writing prompt based on one of the types of writing taught in the unit. These prompts are similar to those found in state writing tests.

The End-of-Year Benchmark Test follows the same design as the Unit Benchmark Tests, but it has more items. It measures selected skills from all six units taught during the year.

The Benchmark Tests are designed to assess student progress at the end of each unit and at the end of the school year. Selections and questions in the Unit Benchmark Tests become progressively more difficult from Unit 1 to Unit 6 to reflect the increasing sophistication of materials students are able to handle.

ADMINISTERING THE TESTS

The Benchmark Tests are designed for group administration. You may decide to administer each test in one sitting, or you may administer parts of the test in two or more sittings. (If you administer the test in two or more sittings, try to schedule the sittings on the same day or within a day of the previous sitting because some of the questions at the end of the test compare and contrast selections.)

These tests were also designed to give teachers the option of separating multiple-choice questions from the constructed-response questions. You may opt to have students skip the constructed-response questions in order to create an all multiple-choice test.

These tests are not intended to be timed. We recommend allowing ample time for all students to complete the tests at their own pace. However, for the purposes of scheduling, planning, and practicing timed-test situations, the chart below shows the number of items in each test part and the estimated amount of time required to complete each part.

Test Part	Number of Items	Estimated Time
Reading – Part 1 (Selection 1)	9 multiple-choice	15 minutes
	1 constructed-response	5 minutes
Reading – Part 1 (Selection 2)	9 multiple-choice	15 minutes
	1 constructed-response	5 minutes
Reading – Part 2 (Vocabulary)	6 multiple-choice	8 minutes
Reading – Part 3 (Phonics)	10 multiple-choice	20–25 minutes
Reading – Part 4 (Writing Conventions) OPTIONAL	6 multiple-choice	8 minutes
Writing – Part 5 OPTIONAL	1 writing prompt	45 minutes

The End-of-Year Benchmark Test has longer selections, sixty multiple-choice items, two constructed-response items, and one writing prompt. To administer the End-of-Year Test, plan on about two hours for Reading – Parts 1–4 and forty-five minutes for Writing – Part 5.

Benchmark Test Teacher's Manual

Directions for Administering the Tests

Before you administer a test . . .

Review the test directions below and on pages T8–T9. Modify the directions as needed based on how you decide to administer each test. For Reading – Parts 1–4, students can mark their responses directly on their tests. In Writing – Part 5, students write compositions in response to a prompt. They write their compositions on the lined pages in their test booklets. You may wish to provide scrap paper that students can use to plan their writing. Only the writing in their test booklets will be scored.

When you are ready to administer a test . . .

Distribute a test to each student. Have students write their name on the front of their test booklets (and on any additional sheets of paper they may use). Have students flip through the test as you point out and explain its key features. For example, point out directions, selection titles, selections, art, Go On and Stop symbols, multiple-choice questions with answer choices, constructed-response questions with lines for written responses, and the writing prompt with a checklist and two lined pages for the composition. Allow time for students to ask any questions they may have about the test's contents before you begin the test.

Directions in **bold** type that follow are intended to be read aloud. Other directions are intended for your information only. For Reading – Part 1, modify the general directions as needed if you intend to skip the constructed-response questions. For Writing – Part 5, you may wish to modify directions regarding the amount of time suggested for the testing session to match the time allowed for your state's writing tests.

Directions for Reading – Part 1: Comprehension

In the first part of this test, you will read two selections and answer some questions about them. There are two types of questions: multiple-choice questions and questions that require you to write short answers.

Mark your answers to the multiple-choice questions in your test. For each question, fill in the circle that goes with the answer you choose. Fill in the circle completely and make your mark heavy and dark. If you want to change your answer, completely erase the mark you made and fill in a different circle. Do not make any other marks in your test.

For Questions A and B, write your answers on the lines in your test. Think carefully and write your ideas as clearly as you can. Allow about five minutes to answer each of these questions.

Read the directions carefully. You can ask me to explain any directions you do not understand. Read the selections and the questions very carefully. You may look back at a selection as often as you like to help you answer the questions.

Answer the questions you are sure about first. If a question seems too difficult, skip it and go back to it later. Check each answer to make sure it is the best answer for the question asked.

Think positively. Some questions may seem hard, but others will be easy. Relax. Most people get nervous about tests. It's natural. Just do your best.

Continue with Reading – Part 1: Comprehension until you come to a STOP sign at the end of Question B. When you have completed that question, put your pencils down, close your test booklets, and look up.

Tell students how much of the test they are expected to complete in this sitting and how much time they have to complete their work. Allow time for students to ask any questions about the directions. Then direct students to open their test booklets to a specified page and begin. You may wish to give students a break upon completion of this part of the test.

Directions for Reading – Parts 2 and 3, and Part 4 (Optional)

Read aloud the directions from the student book for Parts 2, 3, and 4. Tell students how much time they have to complete their work for each part of the test. Point out the STOP signs at the end of each part, instructing them to put their pencils down and look up whenever they come to a STOP sign. That way you can wait for all students to complete the section before moving on to the next part.

Directions for Writing – Part 5 (Optional)

For the last part of the test, you will do a writing exercise. The writing prompt in your test explains what you are going to write about and gives you some ideas for planning your writing. Before you begin writing, think about what you want to say and how you want to say it. You can use scrap paper to jot down your ideas.

After planning what you will write, write your composition on the two lined pages in your test. Be sure that your writing does what the prompt asks you to do. Only the writing in your test booklet will be scored.

Your writing may be about something that is real or make-believe, but remember, you are to write ONLY about the prompt in your test.

You may give your writing a title if you would like. However, a title is not required.

You may NOT use a dictionary. If you do not know how to spell a word, sound out the word and do the best you can.

You may either print or write in cursive. It is important to write as neatly as possible.

Your writing should be easy to read and should show that you can organize and express your thoughts clearly and completely.

I cannot read the prompt to you or help you plan what to write. You must read and plan yourself. Remember to read the prompt first and then plan what you will write.

You have a total of forty-five minutes to read, plan, and respond to your prompt. I will let you know when you have ten minutes left. (You may wish to modify the amount of time you allow for Writing – Part 5 to match the time allowed on your state's writing tests.)

If you finish early, please proofread your composition. Revise and edit the writing in your test. Use the questions in the Checklist for Writers to help you check your composition.

Allow time for students to ask any questions about the directions. Then direct students to open their tests to the writing prompt page, read the prompt, plan their writing, and then write their compositions. Be sure to alert students when they have 10 minutes left.

After testing . . .

Once students are finished testing, collect all test booklets. Directions for scoring the tests begin on page T10. The answer keys begin on page T39. Evaluation charts with alignments to Common Core State Standards (pages T23–T36) are provided along with a class record chart on page T37.

SCORING THE TESTS

The Benchmark Tests are intended to be scored by part—a total score for Reading – Parts 1–4 and a separate score for Writing – Part 5. To make scoring easier, copy and use the following charts as needed:

- the Unit Benchmark Test Evaluation Charts, beginning on page T23, for recording a student's individual scores on a Unit Benchmark Test;

- the End-of-Year Benchmark Test Evaluation Chart, on pages T35 and T36, for recording a student's individual scores on the End-of-Year Benchmark Test; and

- the Class Record Chart, on page T37, for recording test scores for all students for all six units.

Answer keys for each test begin on page T39. In Reading – Part 1, there are two types of items: multiple-choice questions and constructed-response questions. These types of items are scored in slightly different ways, as explained below. In Writing – Part 5, each prompt is linked to one of four different types of writing: narrative, descriptive, expository, or persuasive. For each type of writing, there are four Writing Scoring Rubrics. Each rubric has a different point scale. Choose the rubric that most closely matches the rubric for your state's writing tests or the rubric you deem most appropriate for your students. Writing Scoring Rubrics begin on page T12.

Scoring Multiple-Choice Questions

Each multiple-choice question has four answer choices. The answer keys list the correct answer choice as well as the complete response to each question. Refer to the answer key for the test you are scoring and mark each multiple-choice question as either 1(correct) or 0 (incorrect).

Scoring Constructed-Response Questions

Use the answer keys and the rubric on page T11 to help you score constructed-response questions. Award each constructed-response answer a score from 0 to 2 points, depending on how accurate and complete the response is. The answer keys provide abbreviated descriptions of top responses. Have an ideal top response in your mind before you assess students' responses.

Constructed-Response Scoring Rubric

Points	Description
2	The response indicates a **full understanding** of the question's reading or critical thinking skill. The response is accurate and complete. Necessary support and/or examples are included, and the information is clearly text-based.
1	The response indicates a **partial understanding** of the question's reading or critical thinking skill. The response includes information that is essentially correct and text-based, but it is too general or too simplistic. Some of the support and/or examples may be incomplete or omitted.
0	The response is **inaccurate,** confused, and/or irrelevant, or the student has failed to respond to the task.

Scoring Writing – Part 5

To evaluate students' responses to a writing prompt, familiarize yourself with the writing prompt and review the Writing Scoring Rubrics on pages T12–T19. Identify the type of writing suggested in the writing prompt. (Types of writing for each prompt are identified in the answer keys that begin on page T39.) Then choose one of the four Writing Scoring Rubrics provided for that type of writing. Use the rubric to score each composition on a scale from 1 to 6, 1 to 5, 1 to 4, or 1 to 3.

Writing Scoring Rubrics: Narrative Writing

6-Point Scoring Rubric

6	5	4	3	2	1
narrative writing is well focused on the topic	narrative writing is focused on the topic	narrative writing is generally focused on the topic	narrative writing is generally focused but may stray from the topic	narrative writing is minimally related to the topic	narrative writing is not focused on the topic
contains clear ideas	most ideas are clear	ideas are generally clear	ideas may be somewhat unclear	ideas are often unclear	ideas are unclear
logically organized; uses transitions	logically organized; uses some transitions	logically organized with some lapses; has transitions	somewhat organized; may lack transitions	minimally organized; no transitions	unorganized; no transitions
voice is engaging; well suited to purpose and audience	voice comes through well; suited to purpose and audience	voice comes through occasionally; suited to purpose and audience	voice uneven; not always suited to purpose or audience	slight evidence of voice; little sense of purpose or audience	weak voice; no sense of purpose or audience
demonstrates varied, precise word choice	generally demonstrates varied, precise word choice	often demonstrates varied, precise word choice	word choice could be more varied, precise	poor choice of words; limited vocabulary	limited vocabulary
sentences are complete, fluent, and varied	most sentences are complete and varied	many sentences are complete and varied	some incomplete sentences; little variety	sentences are incomplete; show little or no variety	gross errors in sentence structure; no variety
shows excellent control of writing conventions	shows very good control of writing conventions	shows good control of writing conventions	shows fair control of writing conventions	shows frequent errors in writing conventions	shows many serious errors in writing conventions

5-Point Scoring Rubric

5	4	3	2	1
narrative writing is well focused on the topic	narrative writing is focused on the topic	narrative writing is generally focused on the topic	narrative writing strays from the topic	narrative writing is not focused on the topic
contains clear ideas	most ideas are clear	ideas are generally clear	many ideas are unclear	ideas are unclear
logically organized; uses transitions	logically organized; uses some transitions	logically organized with some lapses; transitions weak	little organization; few or no transitions	unorganized; no transitions
voice is engaging; well suited to purpose and audience	voice is fairly strong; suited to purpose and audience	voice comes through occasionally; may not suit purpose or audience	voice comes through rarely; poorly suited to purpose or audience	weak voice; no sense of audience or purpose
demonstrates varied, precise word choice	generally demonstrates varied, precise word choice	word choice could be more varied, precise	poor choice of words; limited vocabulary	choice of words very limited
sentences are complete, fluent, and varied	most sentences are complete and varied	many sentences are complete; generally varied	incomplete sentences; little variety	incomplete sentences; no variety
shows excellent control of writing conventions	shows very good control of writing conventions	shows fairly good control of writing conventions	shows frequent errors in writing conventions	shows many serious errors in writing conventions

Writing Scoring Rubrics: Narrative Writing

4-Point Scoring Rubric

4	3	2	1
narrative writing is well focused on the topic	narrative writing is focused on the topic	narrative writing may stray from the topic	narrative writing is not focused on the topic
contains clear ideas	most ideas are clear	some ideas may be unclear	ideas are unclear
logically organized; uses transitions	logically organized; uses some transitions	little organization; may be few or no transitions	unorganized; no transitions
voice is engaging; well suited to purpose and audience	voice is fairly strong; suited to purpose and audience	slight evidence of voice; may be poorly suited to purpose or audience	weak voice; no sense of audience or purpose
demonstrates varied, precise word choice	generally demonstrates varied, precise word choice	choice of words limited	choice of words very limited
sentences are complete, fluent, and varied	most sentences are complete and varied	many incomplete sentences; little variety	mostly incomplete sentences; no variety
shows excellent control of writing conventions	shows very good control of writing conventions	shows frequent errors in writing conventions	shows many serious errors in writing conventions

3-Point Scoring Rubric

3	2	1
narrative writing is well focused on the topic	narrative writing is generally focused on the topic	narrative writing is not focused on the topic
contains clear ideas	ideas are sometimes unclear	ideas are unclear
logically organized; uses transitions	logically organized with lapses; transitions need improvement	unorganized; no transitions
voice is engaging; well suited to purpose and audience	voice comes through fairly well; may not suit purpose or audience	weak voice; no sense of audience
demonstrates varied, precise word choice	word choice could be more varied, precise	choice of words very limited
sentences are complete, fluent, and varied	some sentences are complete and varied	incomplete sentences; no variety
shows excellent control of writing conventions	shows fair control of writing conventions	shows many serious errors in writing conventions

Writing Scoring Rubrics: Descriptive Writing

6-Point Scoring Rubric

6	5	4	3	2	1
descriptive writing is well focused on the topic	descriptive writing is focused on the topic	descriptive writing is generally focused on the topic	descriptive writing may stray from the topic	descriptive writing is minimally related to the topic	descriptive writing is not focused on the topic
contains clear ideas	most ideas are clear	ideas are generally clear	ideas may be somewhat unclear	ideas are often unclear	ideas are unclear
logically organized; uses transitions	logically organized; uses some transitions	logically organized with some lapses; has transitions	somewhat organized; may lack transitions	minimally organized; no transitions	unorganized; no transitions
voice is engaging; well suited to purpose and audience	voice comes through well; suited to purpose and audience	voice comes through occasionally; suited to purpose and audience	voice uneven; not always suited to purpose or audience	slight evidence of voice; little sense of purpose or audience	weak voice; no sense of purpose or audience
precise, vivid language paints strong pictures	generally demonstrates varied, precise word choice	often demonstrates varied, precise word choice	word choice could be more varied, precise	poor choice of words; limited vocabulary	limited vocabulary
sentences are complete, fluent, and varied	most sentences are complete and varied	many sentences are complete and varied	some incomplete sentences; little variety	sentences are incomplete; show little or no variety	gross errors in sentence structure; no variety
shows excellent control of writing conventions	shows very good control of writing conventions	shows good control of writing conventions	shows fair control of writing conventions	shows frequent errors in writing conventions	shows many serious errors in writing conventions

5-Point Scoring Rubric

5	4	3	2	1
descriptive writing is well focused on the topic	descriptive writing is focused on the topic	descriptive writing is generally focused on the topic	descriptive writing strays from the topic	descriptive writing is not focused on the topic
contains clear ideas	most ideas are clear	ideas are generally clear	many ideas are unclear	ideas are unclear
logically organized; uses transitions	logically organized; uses some transitions	logically organized with some lapses; transitions weak	little organization; few or no transitions	unorganized; no transitions
voice is engaging; well suited to purpose and audience	voice is fairly engaging; suited to purpose and audience	voice comes through occasionally; may not suit purpose or audience	voice comes through rarely; poorly suited to purpose or audience	weak voice; no sense of audience or purpose
demonstrates varied, precise word choice	generally demonstrates varied, precise word choice	word choice could be more varied, precise	poor word choice; limited vocabulary	word choice very limited
sentences are complete, fluent, and varied	most sentences are complete and varied	many sentences are complete; generally varied	incomplete sentences; little variety	incomplete sentences; no variety
shows excellent control of writing conventions	shows very good control of writing conventions	shows fairly good control of writing conventions	shows frequent errors in writing conventions	shows many serious errors in writing conventions

Writing Scoring Rubrics: Descriptive Writing

4-Point Scoring Rubric

4	3	2	1
descriptive writing is well focused on the topic	descriptive writing is focused on the topic	descriptive writing may stray from the topic	descriptive writing is not focused on the topic
contains clear ideas	most ideas are clear	some ideas may be unclear	ideas are unclear
logically organized; uses transitions	logically organized; uses some transitions	little organization; may be few or no transitions	unorganized; no transitions
voice is engaging; well suited to purpose and audience	voice is fairly engaging; suited to purpose and audience	slight evidence of voice; may be poorly suited to audience or purpose	weak voice; no sense of audience or purpose
demonstrates varied, precise word choice	generally demonstrates varied, precise word choice	choice of words limited	word choice very limited
sentences are complete, fluent, and varied	most sentences are complete and varied	many incomplete sentences; little variety	mostly incomplete sentences; no variety
shows excellent control of writing conventions	shows very good control of writing conventions	shows frequent errors in writing conventions	shows many serious errors in writing conventions

3-Point Scoring Rubric

3	2	1
descriptive writing is well focused on the topic	descriptive writing is generally focused on the topic	descriptive writing is not focused on the topic
contains clear ideas	ideas are sometimes unclear	ideas are unclear
logically organized; uses transitions	logically organized with lapses; transitions need improvement	unorganized; no transitions
voice is engaging; well suited to purpose and audience	voice comes through fairly well; may not suit purpose or audience	weak voice; no sense of purpose or audience
demonstrates varied, precise word choice	word choice could be more varied, precise	choice of words very limited
sentences are complete, fluent, and varied	some sentences are complete and varied	incomplete sentences; no variety
shows excellent control of writing conventions	shows fair control of writing conventions	shows many serious errors in writing conventions

Writing Scoring Rubrics: Expository Writing

6-Point Scoring Rubric

6	5	4	3	2	1
expository writing is well focused on the topic	expository writing is focused on the topic	expository writing is generally focused on the topic	expository writing may stray from the topic	expository writing is minimally related to the topic	expository writing is not focused on the topic
contains clear ideas	most ideas are clear	ideas are generally clear	ideas may be somewhat unclear	ideas are often unclear	ideas are unclear
logically organized; uses transitions	logically organized; uses some transitions	logically organized with some lapses; has transitions	little organization; may lack transitions	minimally organized; no transitions	unorganized; no transitions
voice is engaging; well suited to purpose and audience	voice comes through well; suited to purpose and audience	voice comes through occasionally; suited to purpose and audience	voice uneven; not always suited to purpose or audience	slight evidence of voice; little sense of purpose or audience	weak voice; no sense of purpose or audience
demonstrates varied, precise word choice	generally demonstrates varied, precise word choice	often demonstrates varied, precise word choice	word choice could be more varied, precise	poor choice of words; limited vocabulary	limited vocabulary
sentences are complete, fluent, and varied	most sentences are complete and varied	many sentences are complete and varied	some incomplete sentences; little variety	sentences are incomplete; show little or no variety	gross errors in sentence structure; no variety
shows excellent control of writing conventions	shows very good control of writing conventions	shows good control of writing conventions	shows fair control of writing conventions	shows frequent errors in writing conventions	shows many serious errors in writing conventions

5-Point Scoring Rubric

5	4	3	2	1
expository writing is well focused on the topic	expository writing is focused on the topic	expository writing is generally focused on the topic	expository writing strays from the topic	expository writing is not focused on the topic
contains clear ideas	most ideas are clear	ideas are generally clear	many ideas are unclear	ideas are unclear
logically organized; uses transitions	logically organized; uses some transitions	logically organized with some lapses; transitions weak	little organization; few or no transitions	unorganized; no transitions
voice is engaging; well suited to purpose and audience	voice is fairly engaging; suited to purpose and audience	voice comes through occasionally; may not suit purpose or audience	voice comes through rarely; poorly suited to purpose or audience	weak voice; no sense of audience or purpose
demonstrates varied, precise word choice	generally demonstrates varied, precise word choice	word choice could be more varied, precise	poor word choice; limited vocabulary	word choice very limited
sentences are complete, fluent, and varied	most sentences are complete and varied	many sentences are complete; generally varied	incomplete sentences; little variety	incomplete sentences; no variety
shows excellent control of writing conventions	shows very good control of writing conventions	shows fairly good control of writing conventions	shows frequent errors in writing conventions	shows many serious errors in writing conventions

Benchmark Test Teacher's Manual

Writing Scoring Rubrics: Expository Writing

4-Point Scoring Rubric

4	3	2	1
expository writing is well focused on the topic	expository writing is focused on the topic	expository writing may stray from the topic	expository writing is not focused on the topic
contains clear ideas	most ideas are clear	some ideas may be unclear	ideas are unclear
logically organized; uses transitions	logically organized; uses some transitions	little organization; may be few or no transitions	unorganized; no transitions
voice is engaging; well suited to purpose and audience	voice is fairly engaging; suited to purpose and audience	slight evidence of voice; may be poorly suited to audience or purpose	weak voice; no sense of audience or purpose
demonstrates varied, precise word choice	generally demonstrates varied, precise word choice	choice of words limited	word choice very limited
sentences are complete, fluent, and varied	most sentences are complete and varied	many incomplete sentences; little variety	mostly incomplete sentences; no variety
shows excellent control of writing conventions	shows very good control of writing conventions	shows frequent errors in writing conventions	shows many serious errors in writing conventions

3-Point Scoring Rubric

3	2	1
expository writing is well focused on the topic	expository writing is generally focused on the topic	expository writing is not focused on the topic
contains clear ideas	ideas are sometimes unclear	ideas are unclear
logically organized; uses transitions	logically organized with lapses; transitions need improvement	unorganized; no transitions
voice is engaging; well suited to purpose and audience	voice comes through fairly well; may not suit purpose or audience	weak voice; no sense of purpose or audience
demonstrates varied, precise word choice	word choice could be more varied, precise	choice of words very limited
sentences are complete, fluent, and varied	some sentences are complete and varied	incomplete sentences; no variety
shows excellent control of writing conventions	shows fair control of writing conventions	shows many serious errors in writing conventions

Writing Scoring Rubrics: Persuasive Writing

6-Point Scoring Rubric

6	5	4	3	2	1
persuasive writing is well focused on the topic	persuasive writing is focused on the topic	persuasive writing is generally focused on the topic	persuasive writing is generally focused but may stray from the topic	persuasive writing is minimally related to the topic	persuasive writing is not focused on the topic
contains clear ideas	most ideas are clear	ideas are generally clear	ideas may be somewhat unclear	ideas are often unclear	ideas are unclear
presents reasons in order; uses transitions	presents reasons in some order; uses some transitions	presents most reasons in order; has transitions	reasons may not be in proper order; may lack transitions	reasons are not in order; no transitions	reasons, if any, are not in order; no transitions
voice is engaging; well suited to purpose and audience	voice comes through well; suited to purpose and audience	voice comes through occasionally; suited to purpose and audience	voice uneven; not always suited to purpose or audience	slight evidence of voice; little sense of audience or purpose	weak voice; no sense of purpose or audience
demonstrates precise, persuasive wording	generally demonstrates precise, persuasive word choice	often demonstrates precise, persuasive word choice	word choice is not always precise or persuasive	poor choice of words; not very persuasive	limited vocabulary; fails to persuade
sentences are complete, fluent, and varied	most sentences are complete and varied	many sentences are complete and varied	some incomplete sentences; little variety	sentences are incomplete; show little or no variety	gross errors in sentence structure; no variety
shows excellent control of writing conventions	shows very good control of writing conventions	shows good control of writing conventions	shows fair control of writing conventions	shows frequent errors in writing conventions	shows many serious errors in writing conventions

5-Point Scoring Rubric

5	4	3	2	1
persuasive writing is well focused on the topic	persuasive writing is focused on the topic	persuasive writing is generally focused on the topic	persuasive writing strays from the topic	persuasive writing is not focused on the topic
contains clear ideas	most ideas are clear	ideas are generally clear	many ideas are unclear	ideas are unclear
presents reasons in order; uses transitions	presents reasons in some order; uses some transitions	presents most reasons in order; transitions weak	reasons are not in order; few or no transitions	reasons, if any, are not in order; no transitions
voice is engaging; well suited to purpose and audience	voice is fairly engaging; suited to purpose and audience	voice comes through occasionally; may not suit purpose or audience	voice comes through rarely; poorly suited to audience or purpose	weak voice; no sense of audience or purpose
demonstrates precise, persuasive wording	generally demonstrates precise, persuasive word choice	word choice could be more precise, persuasive	word choice limited; not persuasive	word choice very limited; fails to persuade
sentences are complete, fluent, and varied	most sentences are complete and varied	many sentences are complete; generally varied	incomplete sentences; little variety	incomplete sentences; no variety
shows excellent control of writing conventions	shows very good control of writing conventions	shows fairly good control of writing conventions	shows frequent errors in writing conventions	shows many serious errors in writing conventions

Writing Scoring Rubrics: Persuasive Writing

4-Point Scoring Rubric

4	3	2	1
persuasive writing is well focused on the topic	persuasive writing is focused on the topic	persuasive writing may stray from the topic	persuasive writing is not focused on the topic
contains clear ideas	most ideas are clear	some ideas may be unclear	ideas are unclear
presents reasons in order; uses transitions	presents reasons in some order; uses some transitions	reasons may not be in order; may be few or no transitions	reasons, if any, are not in order; no transitions
voice is engaging; well suited to purpose and audience	voice is fairly engaging; suited to purpose and audience	slight evidence of voice; may be poorly suited to purpose or audience	weak voice; no sense of audience or purpose
demonstrates precise, persuasive wording	generally demonstrates precise, persuasive word choice	choice of words limited; not very persuasive	word choice very limited; fails to persuade
sentences are complete, fluent, and varied	most sentences are complete and varied	many incomplete sentences; little variety	many incomplete sentences; no variety
shows excellent control of writing conventions	shows very good control of writing conventions	shows frequent errors in writing conventions	shows many serious errors in writing conventions

3-Point Scoring Rubric

3	2	1
persuasive writing is well focused on the topic	persuasive writing is generally focused on the topic	persuasive writing is not focused on the topic
contains clear ideas	ideas are sometimes unclear	ideas are unclear
logically organized; presents reasons in order	logically organized with lapses; presents most reasons in order	unorganized; reasons, if any, are not in order
voice is engaging; well suited to purpose and audience	voice comes through fairly well; may not suit audience or purpose	weak voice; no sense of audience or purpose
demonstrates precise, persuasive word choice	word choice could be more precise, persuasive	choice of words very limited; fails to persuade
sentences are complete, fluent, and varied	some sentences are complete and varied	incomplete sentences; no variety
shows excellent control of writing conventions	shows fair control of writing conventions	shows many serious errors in writing conventions

Using the Evaluation Charts

Use the Evaluation Charts beginning on page T23 to score the Unit Benchmark Tests and the End-of-Year Benchmark Test. To score one of these tests, use the following procedure:

1. Make a copy of the appropriate Evaluation Chart for each student.

2. To score Reading – Parts 1–4, circle the score for each item on the Evaluation Chart. Multiple-choice questions are scored 0 (incorrect) or 1 (correct). Constructed-response questions are scored 0, 1, or 2 points. Use the answer key for the test you are scoring and the Constructed-Response Scoring Rubric on page T11 to help you score the Reading parts of the test.

3. Find the student's total score for Reading – Parts 1–4 by adding the individual scores for all items.

4. Use the formula on the Evaluation Chart to find the percentage score for Reading – Parts 1–4 by dividing the total *obtained* score by the total *possible* score and then multiplying the quotient by 100.

5. To score Writing – Part 5, identify the type of writing suggested in the prompt and choose one of the four Writing Scoring Rubrics for that type of writing. Read the student's writing and score each composition on a scale from 1 to 6, 1 to 5, 1 to 4, or 1 to 3.

6. Mark the student's Writing score on the Evaluation Chart. Add any notes or observations about the writing that may be helpful to you and the student in later instruction.

INTERPRETING TEST RESULTS

A student's score on a Benchmark Test provides only one look at the student's progress and should be interpreted in conjunction with other assessments and the teacher's observations. However, a low score on one or both parts of a Benchmark Test probably indicates a need for closer review of the student's performance and perhaps additional instruction.

Regrouping for Instruction

The Benchmark Tests can help you make regrouping decisions. In Grade 3 there are opportunities for regrouping at the end of Units 2, 3, 4, and 5. Depending on each student's progress, teachers may prefer to regroup more or less frequently.

Students who score 65% or below on the multiple-choice items of the Comprehension, Vocabulary, and Phonics sections of the Benchmark Tests and who typically demonstrate unsatisfactory work on assignments and in classroom discussions would benefit from being in the Strategic Intervention reading group for the next unit of instruction.

Students who score between 66% and 90% on the multiple-choice items of the Comprehension, Vocabulary, and Phonics sections of the Benchmark Tests and who meet other criteria, such as consistently satisfactory work on assignments and in classroom discussions, likely belong in the On-Level reading group for the next unit of instruction. Students in the low end of that range should be observed carefully and may need on-going assistance, extra instruction, and opportunities for further practice, just as students in the Strategic Intervention group do. Students in the upper end of that range should receive their instruction and practice with on-level materials, but they may need extra challenge and enrichment, just as students in the Advanced reading group do.

Students who score 91% or above on the multiple-choice items of the Comprehension, Vocabulary, and Phonics sections of the Benchmark Tests and who meet other criteria, such as consistently excellent performance on assigned paperwork and in classroom discussions, are capable of work in the Advanced reading group for the next unit of instruction. They should be given multiple opportunities to engage in enrichment activities and real-world investigations.

Further Analysis of Results

Each Reading (Parts 1–4) item on an Evaluation Chart is linked to a tested skill and a Common Core State Standard. By identifying which items the student answered incorrectly and referring to the list of tested skills, you may be able to determine specific skills or areas in which the student needs additional help. For example, if the student answers six questions incorrectly and several involve literary elements such as plot and character, you may want to plan additional instruction for the student in this area. While the Benchmark Tests do not provide sufficient context coverage of individual skills to be truly "diagnostic," students' performance patterns can often provide useful clues as to particular strengths and weaknesses.

Grading: For more information on how to use a writing assessment scale as an element in determining classroom grades, refer to the "Grading Writing" section of the *Assessment Handbook*.

ASSISTING ENGLISH LANGUAGE LEARNERS

While the Benchmark Tests provide teachers with a way to measure students' progress on a unit-by-unit basis, Benchmark Tests also provide an opportunity for teachers to help English language learners become familiar with the linguistic patterns and structures they will encounter while taking state tests. The format of the Benchmark Tests is similar to the format of the state tests, with similar direction lines, question stems, answer formats, and markings to "stop" and "go on."

Among assessment tools, standardized tests cause teachers of English language learners the most concern. State tests, considered "high stakes," may be used to evaluate the effectiveness of the curriculum, the teacher, or the instructional approach. They are used to evaluate students' overall progress. High-stakes tests are typically designed and normed for proficient speakers of English. By providing opportunities for students to become familiar with the formats and language of the Benchmark Tests, teachers assist English language learners in obtaining results that reflect students' learning of the content rather than their aptitude for reading and comprehending test language. Teachers can use specific strategies to prepare English language learners for assessment. Using these strategies on the Benchmark Tests will increase students' comfort levels and success with assessment tools such as the state tests.

Testing Strategies for All English Language Learners

Provide Accommodations for Students' Success

Any accommodations appropriate for English language learners should address students' linguistic needs, either directly or indirectly. As you consider accommodations for testing, keep in mind that the accommodations that you provide for the Benchmark Tests should be consistent with accommodations that you would provide on the state tests as well. Most importantly, consider, as you make accommodations for English language learners that the ultimate goal is for these students to handle mainstream testing settings, terminology, and instruction, so any accommodations that you provide should be considered stepping stones to students' eventual successful encounter with mainstream testing conditions.

1. Simplify and clarify directions. Providing instructions in simplified formats can reduce the language load for English language learners and help them focus solely on the task and content for the specific question(s). A good rule of thumb is to match the language used with the test to the language used with instruction. Students benefit from your replacing complex English words with simpler English words that they are already familiar with or can grasp more easily. However, it is never appropriate to translate test directions into students' home languages. This practice will not benefit students when they encounter state tests. (*See below* **A Word of Caution**.) However, you may ask students to restate directions in their own words so you are sure they understand them.

2. Provide a setting consistent with the instructional setting. Administering tests in an alternate, smaller, even one-on-one, setting can allow for verbal scaffolding and provide English language learners with a setting that is comfortable and familiar to them. Be sure that the alternate setting is a setting with which students are familiar. Move students to mainstream testing settings as soon as you feel they are ready

3. Consider timing. Provide additional testing time and allow frequent or extended breaks during testing. On the Benchmark Tests, for example, students may benefit from a break between the two Comprehension passage/item sets or after the Comprehension section and before the Vocabulary section. The Writing sections are rigorous for students. Consider completing these portions on a different day or after a significant break. Keep in mind, however, that while this type of accommodation is one that is most often used for English language learners in mainstream classrooms, it is more important to be sure that students are receiving the linguistic support they need.

4. Provide dictionaries. Allow the use of bilingual, word-for-word translation dictionaries as an accommodation for students who are able to use them effectively.

A Word of Caution: In providing accommodations to students, it is important not to compromise the intent of the assessment. It is never appropriate to translate into students' native languages or read aloud in English selections or questions in the Comprehension sections or questions in the Phonics or Writing Convention sections. These practices alter the constructs of the assessments. For example, the reading comprehension assessments are designed to measure both word recognition and understanding, so translating or reading the selections to students actually changes the intent of the tests.

Following the administration of the assessments, it is important to note which accommodations were used for English language learners and to interpret scores with that information in mind. As students progress in their English language skills and become more comfortable with testing, it is important to reconsider accommodations that were provided on previous tests.

Familiarize Students with Academic Language and Test Language

The Benchmark Tests use routine terminology and formats that are designed to mirror the experience of taking state tests. Helping students improve their understanding and use of academic language is an essential way to prepare students for assessment. The practice of "teaching to the test" is often criticized—and rightfully so—but helping English language learners understand the language of tests and other assessment instruments levels the playing field for these students, allowing them to demonstrate what they've learned about the content, rather than struggling with the test language and formats. All students, but especially English language learners, must be taught test-taking strategies and must build background about the language and procedures of taking tests. **What strategies can you explicitly offer to students to prepare for assessment?**

1. Focus on Academic English and Meaningful Oral Language Experiences

Many English language learners may quickly master *social* English, the conversational language skills and conventions used in everyday interactions with classmates. These same learners, however, frequently encounter difficulty with the *academic* English found on formal assessments. Students may also have gaps in understanding between oral and written English. The structure of academic English is complex, e.g., fiction and nonfiction text structures, paragraph organization, and syntax, including prepositional phrases, introductory clauses, and pronoun references. There are structural analysis constraints at the word, sentence, paragraph, and text levels.

Development of academic language is one of the primary sources of difficulty for English language learners at all ages and grades while also being fundamental to all students' success. The vocabulary of academic English consists of specialized meanings of common words, abstract concepts, multiple-meaning words, and words based on Latin and Greek roots. As students read test passages, they may encounter unfamiliar topics and concepts. Recognize that it takes years for students to master academic English, but that you can help them make progress on the way. Highlight and discuss routinely the *academic* language, vocabulary, syntax, and narrative and expository text structures encountered in textbooks and trade books. Remember that academic English is not another name for "standard English." Academic English is the special form of English that is used in the classroom and in written texts. The grammatical constructions, words, and rhetorical conventions are not often used in everyday spoken language. The home language does *not* have to be English in order for students to benefit from experiences in using academic language. If it proves helpful, students may be encouraged to connect what they know in their home languages to what they are learning about academic English.

Provide students with experiences with academic language by reading to them and discussing readings, instructional activities, and experiences. Draw students into instructional conversations focused on the language they encounter in their school texts and other materials to show students how language works. Provide students with ample opportunities to use the language of texts—and tests—in speaking and in writing. Provide regular opportunities for meaningful oral language experiences in which English language learners participate in discussion of important topics and perform the activities required on tests, such as explaining, describing, comparing, and stating and supporting opinions. Encourage them to use vocabulary that will support academic language development in increased opportunities for structured academic talk.

2. Focus on Test Directions.

Help students understand phrases such as "fill in the circle" or "correctly completes" that are often used in test directions. When possible, model tasks and provide verbal directions in simpler, more common English words. Be explicit in your teaching, using the following examples as a guide.

> # Directions
> **Fill in the circle beside your answer choice.**

For the directions above, talk about the phrase "fill in" and the word "beside." Model and gesture how to follow the directions: *I use this page. I find the number of the question. I read the answers. Then I find the circle, here, next to the correct answer and make it dark, or black, with my pencil.* Be sure children understand how to do this clearly and neatly.

> # Directions
> **Which word best completes the sentences?**

For the directions above, talk about the phrase "best completes." Be sure that students understand that for fill-in-the-blank sentences they must *pick the word that makes the sentence sound correct*, or *choose the word that makes sense in the sentence*. Model how to follow the directions.

3. Focus on Terminology and Strategies

Think about terms that will make the most sense to students as you teach. Instead of using the words *directions*, *test*, and *fill in*, for example, you might use common cognates such as *instructions*, *exam*, and *mark*, which translate to most Romance languages (i.e., in Spanish: *instrucciones*, *examen*, and *marca*). However, move students to the original test words as soon as possible.

Pre-teach the "language of tests" encountered in directions and test items, including:

> Question words, such as: *who, what, which, where, when, why, how,* and *what kind*
>
> Emphasis words, such as: *best, better, first, last, not, except, probably, major, main, mainly, both, neither, either, same, different, begin, end, most, mostly,* and *least*
>
> Action words, such as: *explain, compare, describe,* and *discuss*

Words such as *both* and *not* may seem simple, but their uses in test questions often prove otherwise. English language learners need help in seeing how such words frame and constrain ideas expressed in sentences in which they appear.

Throughout the year, students need robust vocabulary instruction in English for additional common test words and phrases such as *test form, test booklet, best describes, base your answer on, author, author's purpose, paragraph, selection, dictionary entry, composition, details, events, results, opposite of, statement of fact* or *opinion,* and *support your answer.* Mine the tests for other words and phrases that are important for students to learn.

Familiarize students with basic test formats, such as multiple choice (4 options) and constructed response items, cloze sentences, underlining of key words and sounds, and writing prompt boxes, so that they develop skills in locating key information. Use released tests or models of tests, providing students with plenty of practice in test formats. Be explicit in your instruction, using the following examples as a guide.

Directions
Choose the word that correctly completes the sentence.

1   **Dogs can be trained to help people who cannot _____ by listening for certain noises.**

     ○ hire

     ○ hair

     ○ hear

     ○ here

Explain the test format: *On some tests, there are sentences with a blank, or empty, line. The line shows a word is missing in the sentence. I need to choose the word that best completes, or finishes, the sentence. This is the word that makes the sentence have the correct meaning.* Model how to complete the sentence.

25 Li sat in his garden and enjoyed a simple <u>supper</u>.

Which word has the same middle sound as the <u>pp</u> in <u>supper</u>?

○ happy

○ dinner

○ rabbit

○ garden

Explain the test format: *Sometimes, test questions have words and letters that are underlined. That means a line is under the words and letters. I pay special attention to words and letters with lines under them. Questions ask about these words and letters. In this question, the words and letters with lines under them have special sounds.* Model how to answer the question. (Note: Reading comprehension selections and vocabulary questions include underlined tested vocabulary words.)

24 In a dictionary a word can have many different meanings. Look at the dictionary definitions below. Which meaning of <u>cone</u> is used in the second selection?

○ a solid object with a flat, round base that narrows to a point at the top

○ anything shaped like a cone, such as an ice-cream cone

○ a kind of cell in the retina of the eye that responds to bright light and color

○ a scaly growth that bears seeds on pine, cedar, fir, and many other evergreen trees

Explain the test format: *Some test questions use a dictionary entry, or definitions (meanings) of a word, to ask me what a word in the selection means. The word is underlined, has a line under it, in the question. Some words have different meanings. The answer choices show the different meanings, or definitions, of the word. I need to choose the right definition. The correct answer is the definition of the word as it is used in the selection.* Model how to complete this type of question.

PROMPT

"Hopping to Freedom" tells about Luke's experience with an animal. Think of an experience you had with an animal. Describe what happened. Give as many details as possible.

Explain the test format: *Some tests ask me to write a composition or a story. At the top of the page is an instruction box, or writing prompt. First I read the instructions in the box to learn what to write about. There are two pages of lines for me to write on.* Explain also the checklist box. *These are questions I read to myself and answer as I check over my writing to make sure it's just the way I want it.*

Model test-taking strategies for students. Help them use their emerging familiarity with high-frequency words and basic language structures in English to select the best answer and eliminate multiple-choice options. Teach students the logic of test questions. Show students, for example, that the question, "Which of the following is *not* a sentence?" entails that all of the listed options except one *are* sentences. Be sure to teach students the types of reading comprehension questions they may encounter on tests. Use released test items or models of test items to provide students with plenty of practice in question types and the test-taking strategies you have taught them. Be explicit in your instruction, using the following examples as a guide.

14 **Why was Chen angry?**

○   His clerks were cheating him.

○   Li's happiness disturbed him.

○   His neighbors were richer than he was.

○   Li made beautiful pots while he made only money.

Model a test-taking strategy for students—underlining key words in the question: *I read the whole selection carefully before I try to answer the questions. What do I do if I can't remember something? Do I guess? No. I can make lines under the important words in the question. Then I can look for these words in the selection and read that part again. This will help me find the correct answer.*

24 **Why did the author most likely write this selection?**
- ○ to get the reader to work hard
- ○ to tell the reader about canaries
- ○ to entertain the reader with an interesting story
- ○ to teach the reader about making pottery

Model test-taking strategies for students—finding the author's purpose through the main idea and genre of the selection and eliminating incorrect answer choices: *I read the whole selection carefully before I try to answer the questions. This question asks about why the author wrote the selection. What is the selection mostly about? A man worries about money. What kind of selection is it? A made-up story. Now I read the answer choices. I try to find three answers that are not correct. The first answer might be correct so I leave that as a choice. I read the other answers. Did the author teach a lot about canaries? No, the selection is a story, not a nonfiction selection with a lot of facts. So, that answer is not correct. I do not choose that answer. Is the story interesting and entertaining, or fun? Yes, so that may be the correct answer. I leave that one for now. Did the author teach a lot about making pottery? No, it is a story, not nonfiction, so that answer is also not correct. Now, which answer is the best answer from the two that are left, the first answer or the third answer? Does the author tell the reader to work hard? No, that is not really the main idea of the story, so that answer is not correct. The third answer is the correct answer.*

PROMPT

Think about Tim from "Rain and Sun and Wind and Snow" and Luke from "Hopping to Freedom." Tell what Tim and Luke might talk about if they met.

Explain how to prepare for a constructed-response question: *I read both selections carefully before I try to answer this question. In this part of the test, I have to write. I read the question in the box to look for words that help me. There are titles from the two stories, so I need to think and write about both stories. I underline the important words in the question. Tim and Luke are the main characters. They each like different things. Tim is interested in the weather, and Luke likes animals. How are they alike? They like nature and the outdoors. That's what they'd talk about!*

Model for students how to read the test itself. Proficient English readers may benefit from strategies such as reading the test question and answer options first and then skimming the passage to find information that will help them select the correct answer to the question. English language learners are not served well by this option. They need to read and understand the passage carefully and then consider how to answer the questions asked. Model this type of test-taking strategy for students as you think aloud and explain the process.

Summarize test formats and strategies for students. Consider making a T-chart to show examples of the question types that students may find on tests. If your T-chart is large enough to be a wall chart, include examples of each type of item from released tests and model tests on the chart. Explain what the structures are and what they ask test-takers to do (or ask students to explain as you teach various strategies).

Evaluation Chart: Grade 3 – Unit 1 Benchmark Test

Student Name _____ **Date** _____

Reading – Parts 1–4				
Item	**Tested Skill**	**Item Type***	**Common Core State Standard**	**Score** (circle one)
Reading – Part 1: Comprehension				
1.	Literary elements: setting	L	Literature 1.	0 1
2.	Literary elements: character	I	Literature 3.	0 1
3.	Literary elements: character	I	Literature 3.	0 1
4.	Sequence	I	Literature 3.	0 1
5.	Sequence	L	Literature 3.	0 1
6.	Draw conclusions	C	Literature 3.	0 1
7.	Sequence	L	Literature 3.	0 1
8.	Literary elements: character	I	Literature 3.	0 1
9.	Literary elements: theme	C	Literature 2.	0 1
A.	Constructed-response text-to-self connection		Writing 10.	0 1 2
10.	Literary elements: character	I	Literature 3.	0 1
11.	Draw conclusions	C	Literature 3.	0 1
12.	Sequence	L	Literature 3.	0 1
13.	Literary elements: character	I	Literature 3.	0 1
14.	Draw conclusions	I	Literature 3.	0 1
15.	Sequence	I	Literature 3.	0 1
16.	Sequence	L	Literature 3.	0 1
17.	Literary elements: theme	C	Literature 2.	0 1
18.	Literary elements: theme	C	Literature 2.	0 1
B.	Constructed-response text-to-text connection		Writing 1.	0 1 2
Reading – Part 2: Vocabulary				
19.	Word structure: suffixes		Language 4.b.	0 1
20.	Word structure: suffixes		Language 4.b.	0 1
21.	Word structure: compound words		Foundational Skills 3.	0 1
22.	Context clues: multiple-meaning words		Language 4.a.	0 1
23.	Dictionary/glossary: unknown words		Language 4.d.	0 1
24.	Word structure: prefixes		Language 4.b.	0 1
Reading – Part 3: Phonics				
25.	Medial consonants: VCCV		Foundational Skills 3.c.	0 1
26.	Plural nouns: -ies		Language 1.b.	0 1
27.	Base words and endings: -ed		Language 1.d.	0 1
28.	Vowel digraphs: ai		Foundational Skills 3.	0 1

Reading – Part 3: Phonics (continued)				
29.	Vowel diphthongs: /ou/ spelled *ou, ow*	Foundational Skills 3.	0	1
30.	Short vowels	Foundational Skills 3.	0	1
31.	Plural nouns: *-es*	Language 2.f.	0	1
32.	Base words and endings: *-er*	Language 1.g.	0	1
33.	Vowel digraphs: *ea*	Foundational Skills 3.	0	1
34.	Vowel diphthongs: /oi/ spelled *oi, oy*	Foundational Skills 3.	0	1
Reading – Part 4: Writing Conventions				
35.	Declarative and interrogative sentences	Language 2.	0	1
36.	Subjects and predicates	Language 1.	0	1
37.	Subjects and predicates	Language 1.	0	1
38.	Declarative and interrogative sentences	Language 2.	0	1
39.	Imperative and exclamatory sentences	Language 2.	0	1
40.	Compound sentences	Language 1.	0	1
Student's Reading Total Score/Total Possible Score _____			/44	

*L = literal   I = inferential   C = critical analysis

Reading – Parts 1–4 percentage score: _____ ÷ 44 = _____ × 100 = _____%

        (student's total score)   (percentage score)

Writing – Part 5	
Writing Score (complete one) _____/6 _____/5 _____/4 _____/3	**Common Core State Standards**
Notes/Observations:	Writing 3. Writing 10. Language 1. Language 2.

Evaluation Chart: Grade 3 – Unit 2 Benchmark Test

Student Name _____ Date _____

Reading – Parts 1–4			
Item	**Tested Skill**	**Item Type***	**Common Core State Standard**	**Score** (circle one)

Item	Tested Skill	Item Type*	Common Core State Standard	Score (circle one)
Reading – Part 1: Comprehension				
1.	Literary elements: character	I	Literature 3.	0 1
2.	Literary elements: setting	C	Literature 1.	0 1
3.	Literary elements: character	I	Literature 3.	0 1
4.	Compare and contrast	I	Literature 3.	0 1
5.	Compare and contrast	I	Literature 3.	0 1
6.	Draw conclusions	C	Literature 3.	0 1
7.	Sequence	L	Literature 3.	0 1
8.	Literary elements: theme	I	Literature 2.	0 1
9.	Compare and contrast	I	Literature 3.	0 1
A.	Constructed-response text-to-world connection		Writing 2.	0 1 2
10.	Main idea and details	I	Informational Text 2.	0 1
11.	Main idea and details	I	Informational Text 1.	0 1
12.	Main idea and details	I	Informational Text 2.	0 1
13.	Main idea and details	L	Informational Text 1.	0 1
14.	Compare and contrast	L	Informational Text 1.	0 1
15.	Main idea and details	I	Informational Text 1.	0 1
16.	Sequence	L	Informational Text 1.	0 1
17.	Draw conclusions	I	Informational Text 1.	0 1
18.	Author's purpose	C	Informational Text 1.	0 1
B.	Constructed-response text-to-text connection		Writing 2.	0 1 2
Reading – Part 2: Vocabulary				
19.	Context clues: synonyms		Language 5.	0 1
20.	Context clues: synonyms		Language 5.	0 1
21.	Context clues: antonyms		Language 5.	0 1
22.	Context clues: synonyms		Language 5.	0 1
23.	Context clues: antonyms		Language 5.	0 1
24.	Context clues: unfamiliar words		Language 4.a.	0 1
Reading – Part 3: Phonics				
25.	Syllables: V/CV		Foundational Skills 3.c.	0 1
26.	Compound words		Foundational Skills 3.c.	0 1
27.	Syllables: VC/V		Foundational Skills 3.c.	0 1
28.	Final syllables: -le		Foundational Skills 3.c.	0 1

Reading – Part 3: Phonics (continued)			
29.	Consonant digraphs: *ph*	Foundational Skills 3.	0 1
30.	Consonant blends: *str*	Foundational Skills 3.	0 1
31.	Compound words	Foundational Skills 3.c.	0 1
32.	Syllables: VC/V	Foundational Skills 3.c.	0 1
33.	Consonant blends: *spl*	Foundational Skills 3.	0 1
34.	Consonant digraphs: *sh*	Foundational Skills 3.	0 1
Student's Regrouping Multiple-Choice Score/Total Possible Score			_____ /34
Reading – Part 4: Writing Conventions			
35.	Irregular plural nouns	Language 1.b.	0 1
36.	Singular possessive nouns	Language 2.d.	0 1
37.	Plural possessive nouns	Language 2.d.	0 1
38.	Common and proper nouns	Language 1.a.	0 1
39.	Singular possessive nouns	Language 2.d.	0 1
40.	Irregular plural nouns	Language 1.b.	0 1
Student's Reading Total Score/Total Possible Score			_____ /44

*L = literal   I = inferential   C = critical analysis

Regrouping (Reading – Parts 1–3) percentage: _____ ÷ 34 = _____ × 100 = _____%
(student's score)   (percentage score)

Reading – Parts 1–4 percentage score: _____ ÷ 44 = _____ × 100 = _____%
(student's total score)   (percentage score)

Writing – Part 5	
Writing Score (complete one) _____/6 _____/5 _____/4 _____/3	**Common Core State Standards**
Notes/Observations:	Writing 2. Writing 10. Language 1. Language 2.

Evaluation Chart: Grade 3 – Unit 3 Benchmark Test

Student Name _____ **Date** _____

Reading – Parts 1–4

Item	Tested Skill	Item Type*	Common Core State Standard	Score (circle one)
Reading – Part 1: Comprehension				
1.	Author's purpose	C	Literature 1.	0 1
2.	Draw conclusions	I	Literature 6.	0 1
3.	Author's purpose	C	Literature 6.	0 1
4.	Draw conclusions	I	Literature 3.	0 1
5.	Sequence	L	Literature 1.	0 1
6.	Draw conclusions	I	Literature 6.	0 1
7.	Draw conclusions	I	Literature 3.	0 1
8.	Compare and contrast	C	Literature 6.	0 1
9.	Literary elements: plot	I	Literature 1.	0 1
A.	Constructed-response text-to-world connection		Writing 2.	0 1 2
10.	Cause and effect	L	Informational Text 3.	0 1
11.	Compare and contrast	I	Informational Text 8.	0 1
12.	Draw conclusions	I	Informational Text 1.	0 1
13.	Cause and effect	I	Informational Text 3.	0 1
14.	Draw conclusions	I	Informational Text 2.	0 1
15.	Author's purpose	C	Informational Text 6.	0 1
16.	Main idea and details	I	Informational Text 2.	0 1
17.	Draw conclusions	I	Informational Text 1.	0 1
18.	Draw conclusions	C	Informational Text 1.	0 1
B.	Constructed-response text-to-text connection		Writing 1.	0 1 2
Reading – Part 2: Vocabulary				
19.	Word structure: suffixes		Language 4.b.	0 1
20.	Compound words		Foundational Skills 3.c.	0 1
21.	Dictionary/glossary: unknown words		Language 4.d.	0 1
22.	Dictionary/glossary		Language 4.d.	0 1
23.	Homonyms		Language 4.	0 1
24.	Context clues: multiple-meaning words		Language 4.a.	0 1
Reading – Part 3: Phonics				
25.	Contractions		Language 2.	0 1
26.	Prefixes: *re-*		Foundational Skills 3.a.	0 1
27.	Consonant sounds: *c* /k/		Foundational Skills 3.	0 1
28.	Suffixes: *-ly*		Foundational Skills 3.a.	0 1

Reading – Part 3: Phonics (continued)			
29.	Consonant patterns: *kn*	Foundational Skills 3.	0 1
30.	Contractions	Language 2.	0 1
31.	Prefixes: *un-*	Language 4.b.	0 1
32.	Consonant sounds: *g* /j/	Foundational Skills 3.	0 1
33.	Suffixes: *-ly*	Foundational Skills 3.a.	0 1
34.	Silent consonant: *st*	Foundational Skills 3.	0 1
Student's Regrouping Multiple-Choice Score/Total Possible Score			____/34
Reading – Part 4: Writing Conventions			
35.	Subject-verb agreement	Language 1.f.	0 1
36.	Subject-verb agreement	Language 1.f.	0 1
37.	Subject-verb agreement	Language 1.f.	0 1
38.	Past, present, and future tense verbs	Language 1.e.	0 1
39.	Past, present, and future tense verbs	Language 1.e.	0 1
40.	Past, present, and future tense verbs	Language 1.e.	0 1
Student's Reading Total Score/Total Possible Score			____/44

*L = literal   I = inferential   C = critical analysis

Regrouping (Reading – Parts 1–3) percentage: _____ ÷ 34 = _____ × 100 = _____%

(student's score) (percentage score)

Reading – Parts 1–4 percentage score: _____ ÷ 44 = _____ × 100 = _____%

(student's total score) (percentage score)

Writing – Part 5	Common Core State Standards
Writing Score (complete one) ____/6 ____/5 ____/4 ____/3	
Notes/Observations:	Writing 2. Writing 10. Language 1. Language 2.

Evaluation Chart: Grade 3 – Unit 4 Benchmark Test

Student Name _____ Date _____

Reading – Parts 1–4

Item	Tested Skill	Item Type*	Common Core State Standard	Score (circle one)
Reading – Part 1: Comprehension				
1.	Main idea and details	I	Informational Text 2.	0 1
2.	Generalize	I	Informational Text 1.	0 1
3.	Fact and opinion	C	Informational Text 1.	0 1
4.	Generalize	I	Informational Text 1.	0 1
5.	Generalize	I	Informational Text 1.	0 1
6.	Generalize	I	Informational Text 1.	0 1
7.	Main idea and details	I	Informational Text 2.	0 1
8.	Author's purpose	C	Informational Text 6.	0 1
9.	Main ideas and details	I	Informational Text 2.	0 1
A.	Constructed-response text-to-world connection		Writing 1.	0 1 2
10.	Cause and effect	L	Informational Text 3.	0 1
11.	Cause and effect	I	Informational Text 3.	0 1
12.	Sequence	I	Informational Text 3.	0 1
13.	Fact and opinion	C	Informational Text 1.	0 1
14.	Sequence	L	Informational Text 3.	0 1
15.	Generalize	I	Informational Text 1.	0 1
16.	Fact and opinion	C	Informational Text 1.	0 1
17.	Draw conclusions	I	Informational Text 1.	0 1
18.	Fact and opinion	C	Informational Text 1.	0 1
B.	Constructed-response text-to-text connection		Writing 2.	0 1 2
Reading – Part 2: Vocabulary				
19.	Context clues: unfamiliar words		Language 4.a.	0 1
20.	Context clues: multiple-meaning words		Language 4.a.	0 1
21.	Word structure: compound words		Foundational Skills 3.c.	0 1
22.	Context clues: synonyms		Language 5.	0 1
23.	Context clues: multiple-meaning words		Language 4.a.	0 1
24.	Context clues: multiple-meaning words		Language 4.a.	0 1
Reading – Part 3: Phonics				
25.	Plurals -f and -fe to v		Language 1.b.	0 1
26.	R-controlled /er/ spelled ur, er		Foundational Skills 3.c.	0 1
27.	Prefixes: pre-		Foundational Skills 3.a.	0 1
28.	Suffixes: -er		Foundational Skills 3.a.	0 1

Reading – Part 3: Phonics (continued)			
29.	Syllable patterns: VCCCV	Foundational Skills 3.c.	0 1
30.	Plurals -f and -fe to v	Language 1.b.	0 1
31.	R-controlled /er/ spelled er	Foundational Skills 3.	0 1
32.	Prefixes: out-	Foundational Skills 3.a.	0 1
33.	Suffixes: -ist	Foundational Skills 3.a.	0 1
34.	Syllable pattern VCCCV	Foundational Skills 3.c.	0 1
Student's Regrouping Multiple-Choice Score/Total Possible Score _____**/34**			
Reading – Part 4: Writing Conventions			
35.	Pronouns	Language 1.f.	0 1
36.	Pronouns	Language 1.f.	0 1
37.	Pronouns	Language 1.f.	0 1
38.	Contractions	Language 2.	0 1
39.	Pronouns	Language 1.	0 1
40.	Prepositions	Language 1.	0 1
Student's Reading Total Score/Total Possible Score _____**/44**			

*L = literal   I = inferential   C = critical analysis

Regrouping (Reading – Parts 1–3) percentage: _____ ÷ 34 = _____ × 100 = _____%
                                      (student's score)   (percentage score)

Reading – Parts 1–4 percentage score: _____ ÷ 44 = _____ × 100 = _____%
                                (student's total score)   (percentage score)

Writing – Part 5	
Writing Score (complete one) _____/6 _____/5 _____/4 _____/3	**Common Core State Standards**
Notes/Observations:	Writing 3. Writing 10. Language 1. Language 2.

Evaluation Chart: Grade 3 – Unit 5 Benchmark Test

Student Name _____   Date _____

Reading – Parts 1–4

Item	Tested Skill	Item Type*	Common Core State Standard	Score (circle one)
Reading – Part 1: Comprehension				
1.	Main idea and details	L	Literature 2.	0 1
2.	Compare and contrast	L	Literature 1.	0 1
3.	Compare and contrast	I	Literature 1.	0 1
4.	Draw conclusions	I	Literature 6.	0 1
5.	Compare and contrast	L	Literature 6.	0 1
6.	Author's purpose	I	Literature 1.	0 1
7.	Draw conclusions	I	Literature 6.	0 1
8.	Compare and contrast	L	Literature 6.	0 1
9.	Draw conclusions	I	Literature 3.	0 1
A.	Constructed-response text-to-self connection		Writing 1.	0 1 2
10.	Fact and opinion	C	Informational Text 1.	0 1
11.	Cause and effect	I	Informational Text 3.	0 1
12.	Main idea and details	I	Informational Text 2.	0 1
13.	Compare and contrast	I	Informational Text 3.	0 1
14.	Author's purpose	C	Informational Text 2.	0 1
15.	Main idea and details	I	Informational Text 2.	0 1
16.	Main idea and details	I	Informational Text 2.	0 1
17.	Draw conclusions	I	Informational Text 1.	0 1
18.	Main idea and details	L	Informational Text 2.	0 1
B.	Constructed-response text-to-text connection		Writing 2.	0 1 2
Reading – Part 2: Vocabulary				
19.	Word structure: compound words		Foundational Skills 3.c.	0 1
20.	Context clues: unfamiliar words		Language 4.a.	0 1
21.	Context clues: homonyns		Language 4.a.	0 1
22.	Context clues: synonyms		Language 5.	0 1
23.	Context clues: unfamiliar words		Language 4.a.	0 1
24.	Context clues: antonyms		Language 5.	0 1
Reading – Part 3: Phonics				
25.	Syllable patterns: CVVC		Foundational Skills 3.c.	0 1
26.	Homophones		Foundational Skills 3.d.	0 1
27.	Vowel sound in *ball*: -al, -aw		Foundational Skills 3.	0 1
28.	Vowel sound in *thought*: -ough, -augh		Foundational Skills 3.	0 1

Reading – Part 3: Phonics (continued)			
29.	Suffixes: *-ment*	Foundational Skills 3.	0 1
30.	Syllable patterns: CVVC	Foundational Skills 3.c.	0 1
31.	Homophones	Foundational Skills 3.	0 1
32.	Vowel sound in *weight*: *a*	Foundational Skills 3.	0 1
33.	Vowel sound in *taught*: *-augh*, *-ough*	Foundational Skills 3.	0 1
34.	Suffixes: *-hood*	Foundational Skills 3.	0 1
Student's Regrouping Multiple-Choice Score/Total Possible Score			**/34**
Reading – Part 4: Writing Conventions			
35.	Adjectives	Language 1.a.	0 1
36.	Adjectives and articles	Language 1.	0 1
37.	Comparative and superlative adjectives	Language 1.g.	0 1
38.	Comparative and superlative adjectives	Language 1.g.	0 1
39.	Comparative and superlative adjectives	Language 1.g.	0 1
40.	Conjunctions	Language 1.h.	0 1
Student's Reading Total Score/Total Possible Score			**/44**

*L = literal   I = inferential   C = critical analysis

Regrouping (Reading – Parts 1–3) percentage: _____ ÷ 34 = _____ × 100 = _____%
     (student's score)   (percentage score)

Reading – Parts 1–4 percentage score: _____ ÷ 44 = _____ × 100 = _____%
     (student's total score)   (percentage score)

Writing – Part 5	
Writing Score (complete one) _____/6 _____/5 _____/4 _____/3	**Common Core State Standards**
Notes/Observations:	Writing 1. Writing 10. Language 1. Language 2.

Evaluation Chart: Grade 3 – Unit 6 Benchmark Test

Student Name _____ **Date** _____

Reading – Parts 1–4

Item	Tested Skill	Item Type*	Common Core State Standard	Score (circle one)
Reading – Part 1: Comprehension				
1.	Cause and effect	L	Literature 1.	0 1
2.	Main idea and details	I	Literature 2.	0 1
3.	Cause and effect	I	Literature 1.	0 1
4.	Draw conclusions	C	Literature 3.	0 1
5.	Cause and effect	I	Literature 1.	0 1
6.	Draw conclusions	I	Literature 3.	0 1
7.	Compare and contrast	C	Literature 1.	0 1
8.	Main idea and details	I	Literature 2.	0 1
9.	Draw conclusions	I	Literature 3.	0 1
A.	Constructed-response text-to-self connection		Writing 2.	0 1 2
10.	Sequence	L	Literature 3.	0 1
11.	Main idea and details	I	Literature 2.	0 1
12.	Literary elements: plot	C	Literature 3.	0 1
13.	Literary elements: plot	L	Literature 3.	0 1
14.	Literary elements: plot	I	Literature 3.	0 1
15.	Literary elements: character	I	Literature 3.	0 1
16.	Literary elements: theme	C	Literature 2.	0 1
17.	Draw conclusions	I	Literature 1.	0 1
18.	Cause and effect	I	Literature 1.	0 1
B.	Constructed-response text-to-text connection		Writing 1.	0 1 2
Reading – Part 2: Vocabulary				
19.	Context clues: antonyms		Language 5.	0 1
20.	Word structure: prefix *un-*		Language 4.b.	0 1
21.	Context clues: antonyms		Language 5.	0 1
22.	Context clues: unknown words		Language 4.a.	0 1
23.	Word structure: suffix *-ful*		Language 4.b.	0 1
24.	Word structure: prefix *dis-*		Foundational Skills 3.a.	0 1
Reading – Part 3: Phonics				
25.	Vowel sounds spelled *oo, ue (tooth/blue)*		Foundational Skills 3.	0 1
26.	Final syllable: *-tion*		Foundational Skills 3.	0 1
27.	Unaccented syllables (schwa)		Foundational Skills 3.	0 1
28.	Prefixes: *im-, in-*		Foundational Skills 3.a.	0 1

Reading – Part 3: Phonics (continued)				
29.	Vowel sounds spelled *oo, u* (*cook*)	Foundational Skills 3.	0	1
30.	Related words	Foundational Skills 3.c.	0	1
31.	Prefixes: *im-, in-*	Foundational Skills 3.a.	0	1
32.	Multisyllabic words with word parts	Foundational Skills 3.c.	0	1
33.	Unaccented syllables (schwa)	Foundational Skills 3.	0	1
34.	Related words	Foundational Skills 3.c.	0	1
Student's Regrouping Multiple-Choice Score/Total Possible Score _____				**/34**
Reading – Part 4: Writing Conventions				
35.	Capitalization	Language 2.	0	1
36.	Punctuation	Language 2.	0	1
37.	Combining sentences	Language 1.h.	0	1
38.	Punctuation	Language 2.	0	1
39.	Punctuation	Language 2.c.	0	1
40.	Combining sentences	Language 1.h.	0	1
Student's Reading Total Score/Total Possible Score _____				**/44**

*L = literal   I = inferential   C = critical analysis

Regrouping (Reading – Parts 1–3) percentage: _____ ÷ 34 = _____ × 100 = _____%
        (student's score)   (percentage score)

Reading – Parts 1–4 percentage score: _____ ÷ 44 = _____ × 100 = _____%
        (student's total score)   (percentage score)

Writing – Part 5	Common Core State Standards
Writing Score (complete one) _____/6 _____/5 _____/4 _____/3	
Notes/Observations:	Writing 3. Writing 10. Language 1. Language 2.

Evaluation Chart: Grade 3 – End-of-Year Benchmark Test

Student Name _____ **Date** _____

Reading – Parts 1–4

Item	Tested Skill	Item Type*	Common Core State Standard	Score (circle one)
Reading – Part 1: Comprehension				
1.	Literary elements: theme	C	Literature 2.	0　1
2.	Draw conclusions	I	Literature 3.	0　1
3.	Main idea and details	I	Literature 2.	0　1
4.	Literary elements: character	I	Literature 3.	0　1
5.	Literary elements: plot	I	Literature 3.	0　1
6.	Author's purpose	C	Literature 6.	0　1
7.	Sequence	I	Literature 3.	0　1
8.	Compare and contrast	I	Literature 3.	0　1
9.	Cause and effect	L	Literature 3.	0　1
10.	Literary elements: character	I	Literature 3.	0　1
11.	Draw conclusions	I	Literature 1.	0　1
12.	Literary elements: character	I	Literature 3.	0　1
13.	Literary elements: plot	I	Literature 3.	0　1
14.	Main idea and details	C	Literature 2.	0　1
15.	Sequence	L	Literature 3.	0　1
16.	Generalize	I	Literature 1.	0　1
17.	Main idea and details	I	Literature 2.	0　1
18.	Author's purpose	C	Literature 6.	0　1
A.	Constructed-response text-to-text connection		Writing 2.	0　1　2
19.	Fact and opinion	C	Informational Text 1.	0　1
20.	Author's purpose	C	Informational Text 6.	0　1
21.	Cause and effect	L	Informational Text 1.	0　1
22.	Cause and effect	L	Informational Text 1.	0　1
23.	Main idea and details	I	Informational Text 2.	0　1
24.	Main idea and details	I	Informational Text 2.	0　1
25.	Draw conclusions	C	Informational Text 1.	0　1
26.	Compare and contrast	I	Informational Text 1.	0　1
27.	Fact and opinion	C	Informational Text 1.	0　1
B	Constructed-response text-to-text connection		Writing 1.	0　1　2
Reading – Part 2: Vocabulary				
28.	Word structure: compound words		Foundational Skills 3.c.	0　1
29.	Word structure: suffix -*ful*		Language 4.b.	0　1
30.	Word structure: prefix *dis-*		Language 4.b.	0　1
31.	Dictionary/glossary: unfamiliar words		Language 4.d.	0　1
32.	Context clues: antonyms		Language 5.	0　1
33.	Context clues: synonyms		Language 5.	0　1
34.	Context clues: unfamiliar words		Language 4.a.	0　1
35.	Context clues: synonyms		Language 5.	0　1
36.	Context clues: homonyms		Language 4.a.	0　1

Reading – Part 3: Phonics

37.	Base words and endings: -ed	Language 2.f.	0 1
38.	Compound words	Foundational Skills 3.c.	0 1
39.	Contractions	Language 2.	0 1
40.	Base words and endings: -ing	Foundational Skills 3.	0 1
41	Vowel sounds spelled *oo, u* (*tooth*)	Foundational Skills 3.	0 1
42.	R-controlled /er/ spelled *ir, ear*	Foundational Skills 3.	0 1
43.	Base words with ending -er and spelling change	Language 1.a.	0 1
44.	Plurals: -s	Language 1.b.	0 1
45.	Consonant sound *ck* /k/	Foundational Skills 3.	0 1
46.	Long vowel digraphs: *ay, ai*	Foundational Skills 3.	0 1
47.	Syllable patterns	Foundational Skills 3.c.	0 1
48.	Vowel sound in *ball*: *aw, au*	Foundational Skills 3.	0 1
49.	Suffixes: -ist	Foundational Skills 3.a.	0 1
50.	Consonant digraphs: *ch*	Foundational Skills 3.	0 1
51.	Silent consonants: *wr*	Foundational Skills 3.	0 1

Reading – Part 4: Writing Conventions

52.	Quotation marks	Language 2.c.	0 1
53.	Past, present, and future verb tenses	Language 1.e.	0 1
54.	Capitalization	Language 2.	0 1
55.	Subject and object pronouns	Language 1.f.	0 1
56.	Possessive pronouns	Language 2.d.	0 1
57.	Verbs	Language 1.d.	0 1
58.	Adjectives and articles	Language 1.	0 1
59.	Subject/verb agreement	Language 1.f.	0 1
60.	Conjunctions and compound sentences	Language 1.h.	0 1
	Student's Reading Total Score/Total Possible Score		_____ /64

*L = literal   I = inferential   C = critical analysis

Reading – Parts 1–4 percentage score: _____ ÷ 64 = _____ × 100 = _____ %
(student's total score)   (percentage score)

Writing – Part 5	
Writing Score (complete one) _____/6 _____/5 _____/4 _____/3	**Common Core State Standards**
Notes/Observations:	Writing 2. Writing 10. Language 1. Language 2.

CLASS RECORD CHART

Grade 3 Unit Benchmark Tests

Teacher Name _____ **Class** _____

Student Name	Unit 1		Unit 2		Unit 3		Unit 4		Unit 5		Unit 6	
	Pt 1–4	Pt 5	Pt 1–4	Pt 5	Pt 1–4	Pt 5	Pt 1–4	Pt 5	Pt 1–4	Pt 5	Pt 1–4	Pt 5
1.												
2.												
3.												
4.												
5.												
6.												
7.												
8.												
9.												
10.												
11.												
12.												
13.												
14.												
15.												
16.												
17.												
18.												
19.												
20.												
21.												
22.												
23.												
24.												
25.												
26.												
27.												
28.												
29.												
30.												

ANSWER KEYS

Unit 1 Benchmark Test

Reading – Part 1: Comprehension

Selection 1: "Baby Bear's Story"

1. fourth choice (a house in the woods)

2. second choice (Baby Bear)

3. third choice (kind)

4. third choice (The door was unlocked.)

5. fourth choice (She ran into the woods.)

6. first choice (He was gald about what they promised to do.)

7. second choice (He sat on the porch.)

8. second choice (He liked her and wanted to play with her.)

9. first choice (You should stay out of strange places.)

A. Use the Constructed-Response Scoring Rubric on page T11 to help you assess students' responses. Assign each response a score from 0 to 2.

A possible top response might be:

I would have liked to make friends with the little bear. But I still would have felt afraid of staying in their home because they were strangers. I would have run outside and back home because it is better to feel safe in your own home.

Selection 2: "Money Means Worries"

10. first choice (working and thinking about money)

11. second choice (Li's happiness disturbed him.)

12. fourth choice (Li was given a bag of coins.)

13. fourth choice (worried and angry)

14. second choice (He gave it back to Chen.)

15. third choice (He worried about what to do with the money.)

16. first choice (Chen felt happy.)

17. third choice (Money does not buy happiness.)

18. third choice (Rich with Happiness)

B. Use the Constructed-Response Scoring Rubric on page T11 to help you assess students' responses. Assign each response a score from 0 to 2.

A possible top response might be:

"Money Means Worries" is like a real-life story. People sometimes get a lot of money that they don't expect. They might not know what to do with it. Then they have to figure out how to spend it in good ways.

Reading – Part 2: Vocabulary

19. third choice (in a cautious way)

20. fourth choice (without harm)

21. second choice (eyelids)

22. fourth choice (simple)

23. first choice (*tray* and *treat*)

24. first choice (not locked)

Reading – Part 3: Phonics

25. first choice (open)

26. second choice (canaries)

27. third choice (lived)

28. fourth choice (face)

29. first choice (cow)

30. second choice (must)

31. first choice (porches)

32. fourth choice (sadder)

33. third choice (three)

34. first choice (toys)

Reading – Part 4: Writing Conventions

35. fourth choice (Are you ready?)

36. third choice (has a new pet hamster)

37. second choice (Sam)

38. fourth choice (What time is it)

39. first choice (Put away your books.)

40. first choice (My brother likes swimming, but I like hiking.)

Writing – Part 5

Prompt: The student is asked to write a story about a day when something interesting happened to him or her.

Scoring: Use one of the Narrative Writing Scoring Rubrics on pages T12–T13 to help you assess students' compositions. Choose one of the four rubrics, and assign each composition a score based on the 6-point, 5-point, 4-point, or 3-point scale.

Unit 2 Benchmark Test

Reading – Part 1: Comprehension

Selection 1: "The Ant and the Dove"

1. fourth choice (clever and kind)

2. first choice (the fountain)

3. second choice (smart and caring)

4. first choice (They were good at solving problems.)

5. third choice (the dove could fly, but the ant could not.)

6. fourth choice (to repay the dove for helping him)

7. second choice (The ant fell into the water.)

8. third choice (Treat others as you would like to be treated.)

9. third choice (were willing to help others.)

A. Use the Constructed-Response Scoring Rubric on page T11 to help you assess students' responses. Assign each response a score from 0 to 2.

A possible top response might be:

The lesson is one good turn deserves another. When someone does something nice for you, you should do something nice for that person. The ant was glad to rescue the dove since the dove had first rescued him.

Selection 2: "James Naismith's Problem"

10. second choice (invented basketball to solve a problem.)

11. first choice (He needed a new game to keep his students under control.)

12. second choice (how Naismith came up with a new game.)

13. fourth choice (The players got hurt.)

14. first choice (They used a ball.)

15. third choice (he didn't want players to get hurt.)

16. second choice (He tried soccer and football indoors.)

17. fourth choice (very pleased)

18. third choice (to tell the reader how basketball began)

B. Use the Constructed-Response Scoring Rubric on page T11 to help you assess students' responses. Assign each response a score from 0 to 2.

A possible top response might be:

The ant and the dove were like James Naismith because all three had to solve a problem. The ant and the dove had to figure out how to save each other. In the story each one was in danger and needed help. James Naismith had to figure out how to invent a new kind of game.

Reading – Part 2: Vocabulary

19. first choice (walk)
20. second choice (fell)
21. fourth choice (loud)
22. third choice (make)
23. second choice (boring—interesting)
24. fourth choice (stated)

Reading – Part 3: Phonics

25. second choice (stu/dent)
26. fourth choice (outdoor)
27. third choice (dam/aged)
28. first choice (ma/ple)
29. third choice (fountain)
30. second choice (restring)
31. first choice (football)
32. third choice (sec/ond)
33. fourth choice (splendid)
34. first choice (washing)

Reading – Part 4: Writing Conventions

35. first choice (deer)
36. third choice (the man's net)
37. fourth choice (the students' behavior)
38. third choice (December)
39. second choice (dove's)
40. first choice (feet)

Writing – Part 5

Prompt: The student is asked to write a paragraph describing how to do something he or she knows how to do, explaining it to someone else.

Scoring: Use one of the Expository Writing Scoring Rubrics on pages T16–T17 to help you assess students' compositions. Choose one of the four rubrics, and assign each composition a score based on the 6-point, 5-point, 4-point, or 3-point scale.

Unit 3 Benchmark Test

Reading – Part 1: Comprehension

Selection 1: "Thinking Like Fred"

1. fourth choice (entertain the reader with a story about a dog.)
2. second choice (tries hard to understand Fred.)
3. second choice (to show that Fred was usually a happy dog)
4. fourth choice (he was thinking.)
5. first choice (Fred refused to get on the elevator.)
6. third choice (couldn't understand how the elevator worked.)
7. first choice (likes to make sense of things.)
8. second choice (before and after his first elevator ride.)
9. third choice (Fred would not get back on the elevator.)

A. Use the Constructed-Response Scoring Rubric on page T11 to help you assess students' responses. Assign each response a score from 0 to 2.

A possible top response might be:

I know dogs can learn tricks and can find their way home when they get lost. They must be smart to do that.

Selection 2: "Service Dogs"

10. first choice (The dog touches its owner.)
11. second choice (what service dogs do for people who are hearing-impaired and for people who cannot walk.)
12. third choice (patient.)
13. fourth choice (The dog will do it again.)
14. fourth choice (so the person and the dog can learn to work together)
15. first choice (to give facts about dogs that help people)

16. fourth choice ("Working Dogs")

17. second choice (thankful)

18. third choice (they care about helping animals as well as people.)

B. Use the Constructed-Response Scoring Rubric on page T11 to help you assess students' responses. Assign each response a score from 0 to 2.

A possible top response might be:

Yes, because the narrator wants to learn all about dogs, and the information in the second selection is very interesting.

Reading – Part 2: Vocabulary

19. fourth choice (helping)

20. fourth choice (grandmother)

21. first choice (candy—cannon.)

22. third choice (glossary.)

23. third choice (hear)

24. third choice (from the beginning to the end of)

Reading – Part 3: Phonics

25. third choice (didn't)

26. second choice (write again)

27. fourth choice (kept)

28. first choice (high)

29. second choice (nation)

30. fourth choice (He had)

31. first choice (unusual)

32. fourth choice (intelligent)

33. third choice (happy)

34. second choice (sand)

Reading – Part 4: Writing Conventions

35. first choice (eat)

36. second choice (is)

37. third choice (are)

38. third choice (went)

39. second choice (played)

40. fourth choice (will be)

Writing – Part 5

Prompt: The student is asked to compare and contrast two people he or she knows or knows about.

Scoring: Use one of the Expository Writing Scoring Rubrics on pages T16–T17 to help you assess students' compositions. Choose one of the four rubrics, and assign each composition a score based on the 6-point, 5-point, 4-point, or 3-point scale.

Unit 4 Benchmark Test

Reading – Part 1: Comprehension

Selection 1: "Art Cars"

1. second choice ("Crazy Cars")

2. second choice (decorate their cars for fun and to be different.)

3. third choice (It's fun to make something no one else has.)

4. fourth choice (Most of them are creative.)

5. third choice (are unlike any other car.)

6. third choice (Some art cars are painted bright colors.)

7. fourth choice (McNally's Plaidmobile.)

8. first choice (to get the reader's attention)

9. third choice (Houston's art car parade has grown over the years.)

A. Use the Constructed-Response Scoring Rubric on page T11 to help you assess students' responses. Assign each response a score from 0 to 2.

A possible top response might be:

I think they would be different and creative. They would be very interesting and have colorful personalities. They would like getting attention and working on projects.

Selection 2: "Making Paper"

10. third choice (to turn the paper and flowers into pulp)

11. second choice (soften.)

12. fourth choice (Get the screen ready.)

13. first choice (Dried flowers are a nice addition, as are pieces of tin foil.)

14. third choice (The paper is put into a blender filled with warm water.)

15. second choice (Some writers like to make their own paper.)

16. first choice (Dye makes the pages beautiful.)

17. fourth choice (there are many materials to gather before making paper.)

18. third choice (Make paper by using the steps described.)

B. Use the Constructed-Response Scoring Rubric on page T11 to help you assess students' responses. Assign each response a score from 0 to 2.

A possible top response might be:

Both people who make paper and people who make art cars like art. They like to make things with their hands. They like to make things that no one else has. The things they make are interesting. People who make paper and people who make art cars work hard to do what they do.

Reading – Part 2: Vocabulary

19. first choice (picture)

20. second choice (changed)

21. third choice (grasshopper)

22. first choice (real)

23. third choice (a wire frame)

24. first choice (pieces of paper)

Reading – Part 3: Phonics

25. third choice (loaves.)

26. first choice (fern)

27. fourth choice (already paid)

28. first choice (one who teaches)

29. third choice (hun/dred)

30. fourth choice (lives)

31. first choice (bird)

32. second choice (do more than)

33. fourth choice (art)

34. third choice (com/plete/ly)

Reading – Part 4: Writing Conventions

35. second choice (They)

36. first choice (me)

37. third choice (Her)

38. fourth choice (He's)

39. third choice (Eric and I went to the library.)

40. third choice (to)

Writing – Part 5

Prompt: The student is asked to write a story about a time he or she made something special.

Scoring: Use one of the Narrative Writing Scoring Rubrics on pages T12–T13 to help you assess students' compositions. Choose one of the four rubrics, and assign each composition a score based on the 6-point, 5-point, 4-point, or 3-point scale.

Unit 5 Benchmark Test

Reading – Part 1: Comprehension

Selection 1: "Old Photographs"

1. third choice ("My Great-Grandfather and Me")

2. second choice (their colors)

3. third choice (They show people having fun.)

4. first choice (liked going on trips.)

5. third choice (The great-grandfather's family trips seemed more enjoyable.)

6. fourth choice (to tell the size of the feather)

7. first choice (that he is like his great-grandfather)

8. second choice (The great-grandfather was dressed up, but the narrator was not dressed up.)

9. second choice (He is curious about his great-grandfather's life.)

A. Use the Constructed-Response Scoring Rubric on page T11 to help you assess students' responses. Assign each response a score from 0 to 2.

A possible top response might be:

It was fun to look at the old postcards. I learned how people dressed in the old days. They told me about the things my great-grandfather did when he was young. The pictures showed me that I even look like him.

Selection 2: "Pet Photography"

10. fourth choice (The best pictures tell a story.)

11. third choice (to get the animal to be still)

12. second choice (how to take pictures of pets.)

13. second choice (It will be from another point of view.)

14. second choice (to give some ideas for photographing pets)

15. fourth choice (If you rub food behind one animal's ear, another animal will cuddle close to it.)

16. first choice (the importance of knowing the pets you are photographing.)

17. fourth choice (clever.)

18. second choice ("Taking Good Pictures of Pets")

B. Use the Constructed-Response Scoring Rubric on page T11 to help you assess students' responses. Assign each response a score from 0 to 2.

A possible top response might be:

Good pictures tell a story and bring back special memories. They show important family members and pets. Good pictures show the personality of the person or pet.

Reading – Part 2: Vocabulary

19. first choice (bulldog)

20. third choice (bend low)

21. second choice (a round toy)

22. first choice (scrapbooks)

23. fourth choice (disagreeable)

24. second choice (rear)

Reading – Part 3: Phonics

25. fourth choice (cur/i/ous)

26. second choice (won)

27. fourth choice (awful)

28. first choice (caught)

29. second choice (announce)

30. third choice (cre/a/ted)

31. first choice (their)

32. third choice (game)

33. fourth choice (daughter)

34. first choice (neighbor)

Reading – Part 4: Writing Conventions

35. third choice (funny)

36. first choice (The boy told a story about an elephant.)

37. second choice (Ray is taller than Nick.)

38. third choice (Beth is the kindest person in my class.)

39. first choice (My mom can walk faster than my dad.)

40. fourth choice (We can stay awake or go to sleep.)

Writing – Part 5

Prompt: The student is asked to write a letter to the local library explaining why it is important to keep old photos of the city that the library is planning to throw away.

Scoring: Use one of the Persuasive Writing Scoring Rubrics on pages T18–T19 to help you assess students' compositions. Choose one of the four rubrics, and assign each composition a score based on the 6-point, 5-point, 4-point, or 3-point scale.

Unit 6 Benchmark Test

Reading – Part 1: Comprehension

Selection 1: "Rain and Sun and Wind and Snow"

1. first choice (the weather there stays cold for a long time.)

2. second choice ("If It's Weather, Tim Loves It")

3. third choice (He saw the weather forecast.)

4. fourth choice (his knowledge of weather)

5. third choice (he would not feel safe outside.)

6. first choice (a tornado)

7. second choice (harsh)

8. third choice (heat and lack of rain)

9. third choice (He spends a lot of time learning about the weather.)

A. Use the Constructed-Response Scoring Rubric on page T11 to help you assess students' responses. Assign each response a score from 0 to 2.

A possible top response might be:

When it is nice outside, I like to ride my bike, just like Tim does in the story. Iris probably never needs an umbrella where she lives. We get lots of rain, so I use my umbrella all the time. I have to wear sunscreen when it is sunny too. It gets really cold here in the winter, so I have to wear a lot of clothes, just like Carl does.

Selection 2: "Hopping to Freedom"

10. third choice (Luke found a baby rabbit.)

11. first choice (a boy who finds an animal but cannot keep it.)

12. second choice (A baby rabbit was hurt.)

13. fourth choice (Mrs. Hurley told Luke why he could not keep the rabbit.)

14. third choice (The rabbit was cared for and then set free.)

15. first choice (kind)

16. second choice (All living things need to be free.)

17. fourth choice (caring.)

18. fourth choice (it did not run away.)

B. Use the Constructed-Response Scoring Rubric on page T11 to help you assess students' responses. Assign each response a score from 0 to 2.

A possible top response might be:

Tim and Luke might talk about nature. They might talk about how interesting it is to observe things in nature. They might tell each other that they want to be some kind of scientist when they grow up.

Reading – Part 2: Vocabulary

19. second choice (bored)
20. third choice (not usual)
21. first choice (dull)
22. fourth choice (healed)
23. third choice (full of help.)
24. second choice (dislike)

Reading – Part 3: Phonics

25. second choice (clue)
26. third choice (expression)
27. fourth choice (above)
28. second choice (impossible)
29. fourth choice (push)
30. second choice (nature)
31. first choice (inexpensive)
32. third choice (re/play/ing)
33. first choice (banana)
34. third choice (impatience)

Reading – Part 4: Writing Conventions

35. second choice (I was in Texas in July and August.)
36. first choice (My teacher is Mr. Jones.)
37. third choice (Tim cleans his room and plays soccer on Saturdays.)
38. first choice (Tim tracks the weather in Marquette, Phoenix, and his hometown in Nebraska.)
39. first choice (Tim says, "Iris and Carl are my cousins.")
40. fourth choice (Jan and Roy like to read.)

Writing – Part 5

Prompt: The student is asked to describe an experience he or she had with an animal.

Scoring: Use one of the Descriptive Writing Scoring Rubrics on pages T14–T15 to help you assess students' compositions. Choose one of the four rubrics, and assign each composition a score based on the 6-point, 5-point, 4-point, or 3-point scale.

End-of-Year Benchmark Test

Reading – Part 1: Comprehension

Selection 1: "Best Friends Do Everything Together"

1. fourth choice (Good friends can like different things.)
2. third choice (They both were talented in their own way.)
3. fourth choice (how friends solved a problem.)
4. first choice (cared about their friendship.)
5. second choice (They agreed to support each other's hobbies.)
6. third choice (tell an entertaining story about friendship.)
7. third choice (The girls signed up for baseball.)
8. fourth choice (Megan was a good athlete, and Jackie was a good singer.)
9. fourth choice (she had done well at baseball practice.)

Selection 2: "We Can Still Be Friends"

10. third choice (She had the idea to play chess through the mail.)
11. fourth choice (patient.)

12. second choice (he could make new friends and keep his old friend.)

13. third choice (Christopher was moving far away from Rachel.)

14. second choice ("A Different Way to Play Chess")

15. first choice (Christopher sent Rachel a letter.)

16. third choice (Rachel and Christopher always shared everything about their day.)

17. third choice (Christopher and Rachel were best friends who loved to play chess.)

18. first choice (to explain how Rachel got the idea to play chess by mail)

A. Use the Constructed-Response Scoring Rubric on page T11 to help you assess students' responses. Assign each response a score from 0 to 2.

A possible top response might be:

Both sets of friends cared about each other. They each came up with a plan to stay friends, even when they wouldn't be together all the time. In both stories, they were worried about staying friends, but it all worked out okay.

Selection 3: "Chess"

19. second choice (Chess is a very exciting game.)

20. fourth choice (give readers facts about chess.)

21. first choice (it cannot move very far at one time.)

22. second choice (chess players need to be good thinkers.)

23. fourth choice (The object of the game is to capture the opposing king.)

24. third choice (the roles of the different chessmen)

25. first choice (it can take years to become a good chess player.)

26. second choice (are played on a board with sixty-four squares.)

27. fourth choice (It contains mostly statements of fact.)

B. Use the Constructed-Response Scoring Rubric on page T11 to help you assess students' responses. Assign each response a score from 0 to 2.

A possible top response might be:

I think Rachel and Christopher liked chess because it is a two-person game that takes a lot of time, and they were best friends who liked to spend time together. Chess is a quiet game that can be played indoors in bad weather. It takes patience and planning, and Christopher and Rachel had to plan and be patient to play through the mail.

Reading – Part 2: Vocabulary

28. third choice (everything)

29. third choice (full of power)

30. second choice (without belief)

31. first choice (degree—delightful.)

32. fourth choice (cheerful)

33. third choice (winner)

34. first choice (eager)

35. second choice (skilled)

36. third choice (a wooden club)

Reading – Part 3: Phonics

37. fourth choice (batted)
38. third choice (headache)
39. first choice (you are)
40. first choice (laugh)
41. third choice (tune)
42. second choice (heard)
43. fourth choice (happier)
44. first choice (neighbors)
45. fourth choice (like)
46. second choice (paid)
47. third choice (pho/to)
48. third choice (pause)
49. first choice (insist)
50. third choice (rich)
51. third choice (ring)

Reading – Part 4: Writing Conventions

52. third choice ("I like to read books," said Lisa.)
53. fourth choice (played)
54. third choice (monday)
55. second choice (him)
56. fourth choice (Shawn and Grace collect coins in their spare time.)
57. second choice (is)
58. fourth choice (I drank a glass of milk and ate an egg.)
59. third choice (Sam and Jon draw while their sister reads.)
60. first choice (Terry likes apples, but she hates oranges.)

Writing – Part 5

Prompt: The student is asked to write a report explaining how to play a game that he or she has learned.

Scoring: Use one of the Expository Writing Scoring Rubrics on pages T16–T17 to help you assess students' compositions. Choose one of the four rubrics, and assign each composition a score based on the 6-point, 5-point, 4-point, or 3-point scale.

OPTIONAL — FLUENCY CHECKS OR RUNNING RECORDS

How to Administer and Score a Fluency Test

A fluency test measures a student's reading rate, or the number of words read correctly per minute (wcpm), on grade-level text the student has not seen before. Give the student a copy of the Student Copy of the passage for the test and make a copy of the Teacher Copy for yourself, noting the formula for calculation at the bottom of the page. (The Teacher Copy has a scale of running numbers to make it easier for you to know how many words the student read during the fluency check, while the passage on the Student Copy does not have the numbers.) Make sure you have put the student's name and the test date at the top of your copy of the passage. Have a watch or clock with a second hand available for timing the reading.

Have the student read the text aloud. Do not have the student read the title as part of the fluency reading; it is not included in the running word count. (You may want to tape-record the student's reading for later evaluation.) Stop the student at exactly one minute and note precisely where the student stopped.

As the student reads orally, on your copy of the text, mark any miscues or errors the student makes during the reading (see the chart on page T50). Count the total number of words the student read in one minute. Subtract any words the student read incorrectly. Record the words correct per minute (wcpm) score on the test.

The formula is: Total # of words read – # of errors = words correct per minute (wcpm).

How to Identify Reading Miscues/Errors

Using the passage on page T51, the chart below shows the kinds of miscues and errors to look for as a student reads aloud, and the notations to use to mark them.

Reading Miscue	Notations
Omission The student omits words or word parts.	Sanya had to write a report for her science class about a planet she ⟨had⟩ never visited.
Substitution The student substitutes words or parts of words for the words in the text.	Sanya's mom came into ~~the~~ *her* room.
Insertion The student inserts words or parts of words that are not in the text.	Sanya was tired of looking at her screen and turned to *around* look out the window. ∧
Mispronunciation/Misreading The student pronounces or reads a word incorrectly.	I can't think of a better way to learn about a ~~place~~ planet.
Hesitation The student hesitates over a word, and the teacher provides the word.	It was raining on Planet Oc̲t̲or.
Self-correction The student reads a word incorrectly but then corrects the error.	Mom ag⟨re⟩ed, so they jumped into their spaceship and headed for Earth.

Notes

- If the student hesitates over a word, wait several seconds before telling the student what the word is.

- If a student makes the same error more than once, count it as only one error.

- Self-correction is not counted as an actual error. However, writing "SC" over the word or words will help you identify words that give the student some difficulty.

Sample Fluency Test

Here is the passage marked as shown on the chart on the previous page. As the student reads the passage aloud to you, mark miscues and errors. Have the student read for exactly one minute, and then mark the last word the student reads.

Student Name _Susan_   Date _9/7/2011_

Sanya's Science Report

92

around
Sanya was tired of looking at her screen and turned ^ to look out the window. It   16

H
was raining on Planet Octor. Sanya had to write a report for science class about a   32

planet she (had) never visited.   37

her
Sanya's mom came into ~~the~~ room. "Why aren't you reading your teaching   49

screen?" she asked.   52

"Oh, I have been. I've decided to write about Earth," Sanya said. "Why don't we   67

place
go there? I can't think of a better way to learn about a planet."   81

(sc)
Mom agreed, so they jumped into their spaceship and headed for Earth. Sanya   94

looked out the / window as they traveled. She recognized Norbeed, a red planet she   108

and her family had visited on vacation. It still had a red halo around it.   123

97 − 5 = 92

Interpreting the Results

According to published norms for oral reading fluency, students at the end of Grade 3 should be reading fluently at 120 words correct per minute in text that is on grade level. This chart gives recommended progress toward that goal.

End of Unit/Grade		Reading Rate (wcpm)
Grade 3	Unit 1	80 to 90
Grade 3	Unit 2	85 to 95
Grade 3	Unit 3	90 to 100
Grade 3	Unit 4	95 to 105
Grade 3	Unit 5	102 to 112
Grade 3	Unit 6	110 to 120
End-of-Year Goal		120

If a student's reading rate is lower than the suggested progress toward the standard for his or her grade level, your notes on the student's miscues may help you determine why the rate is low. Does the student make errors that indicate his or her decoding skills are poor? If so, further instruction in phonics may be needed. Do the errors reflect a lack of comprehension or limited vocabulary? In that case, instruction in comprehension strategies and exposure to more vocabulary words may help. A lack of fluency may indicate a lack of exposure to models of fluent oral reading. It may also mean that the student isn't reading enough material at his or her reading level.

How to Take a Running Record

A Running Record is an assessment of oral reading accuracy and oral reading fluency. A student's reading accuracy is based on the number of words read correctly. This measure is determined by an analysis of the errors a student makes—a miscue analysis. Reading fluency is based on reading rate (the number of words read per minute) and the degree to which the student reads with a "natural flow."

A Running Record may be taken using any reading passage at any time. However, the most valid and reliable assessment fulfills these requirements: (1) the text is appropriate to the student's reading level and interest; and (2) the text is unfamiliar to the student. The passages in this section are well suited for use as either a Fluency Test or a Running Record because they fit these requirements. For additional oral reading accuracy and fluency checks that involve a Running Record, you may choose other passages from grade-level appropriate texts.

The Running Record may be used to verify instructional decisions suggested by other assessments, such as a Placement or Benchmark Test. It may also be used to identify a student's particular strengths and weaknesses in reading and language development. In addition, the Running Record may be administered periodically throughout the year as a means of monitoring student progress.

Measuring oral reading accuracy and oral reading fluency may be accomplished in a single reading, but two different operations are required. The guidelines on pages T54 and T55 explain how to determine each measurement.

How to Measure Oral Reading Accuracy

1. Choose an appropriate grade-level text of about 100 to 200 words, or use those passages that have been provided for use as a Fluency Test.

2. Make copies of the text—one of the Student Copy for the student and one of the Teacher Copy for you. If the text appears in a book, you may have the student read the text from the book.

3. Give the text to the student and have the student read the text aloud. (You may want to tape-record the student's reading for later evaluation. This approach can be especially helpful if you are timing the student's reading or conducting other assessments at the same time.)

4. Your hand should always be "running" on your copy of the text. Put a checkmark above every word the student reads correctly. Mark any miscues or errors the student makes during the reading (see the explanation of reading miscues/errors for Fluency Tests beginning on page T50).

5. Count the total number of errors the student makes and find the percentage score for the number of errors. If you are using a fluency/running record passage from this book, the total word count is indicated for each passage and a formula for determining a percentage score is provided.

6. If you are using a text from a different source, use this formula to get a percentage score:

$$\frac{\text{Total \# of words minus \# of errors}}{\text{Total \# of words}} \times 100 = \text{percentage score}$$

Example: Suppose a student reads a text of 110 words and makes 6 errors.

$$\frac{110 - 6 = 104 \text{ words}}{110} = 0.945 \qquad 0.945 \times 100 = 94.5\% \text{ (round to 95\%)}$$

The percentage score indicates the student's oral reading accuracy (percentage of words in the passage read correctly).

How to Measure Reading Rate

Reading rate is generally defined as number of words per minute (wpm). To determine the reading rate, follow steps 1–3 as described on page T54. Note the exact time when the student begins reading and the time when he or she finishes.

To calculate the number of words per minute, use the formula below:

$$\frac{\text{Total \# of words read}}{\text{\# of seconds}} \times 60 = \text{words per minute}$$

Example: Suppose a student reads a passage of 120 words in 90 seconds.

$$\frac{120}{90} = 1.33 \text{ (round to the nearest hundredth)}$$

1.33 x 60 = 79.8 words per minute (round to 80 wpm)

Interpreting the Results

For oral reading accuracy, use the following criteria:

- A student who reads 98%–100% of the words correctly is reading at an independent level and may need more challenging texts.

- A student who reads 91%–97% of the words correctly is reading at an instructional level and will likely benefit from guided on-level instruction in the regular program.

- A student who reads with an accuracy of 90% or less is reading at a frustration level and may benefit most from targeted instruction with lower-level texts or strategic intervention.

For any student whose Running Record results are not clearly definitive, we recommend administering additional individual assessments, such as classroom observations and anecdotal records. For more information about other assessments, refer to the *Assessment Handbook*.

On the following pages you will find passages that may be used for either Fluency or Running Record Tests. Both a Teacher Copy and a Student Copy have been provided.

Student Name _____ Date _____

Rabbit's Tail

Two little long-tailed rabbits sat beside the river. A large turtle was in the water,	15
warming her shell in the sun.	21
"The grass is greener on the other side," said one rabbit.	32
"I know how we can get across," said the other. He called out, "Auntie Turtle!	47
I was told your family was bigger than mine, but I do not believe it."	62
"It's true," she said. She offered to have her whole family float there in the river	78
so the rabbit could count them. Then the rabbit gathered his whole family on	92
the bank of the river so Auntie could count them.	102
When all the turtles were floating in a line across the river, the rabbits hopped	117
across them to the other side. "Ha!" cried the rabbit. "We fooled you into helping us	133
cross the river!"	136
The rabbits began nibbling the grass and did not see Auntie Turtle crawling as	150
fast as she could up the bank. She snapped their tails off as punishment for fooling	166
her. And that is why a rabbit now has a fluffy ball where a tail used to be.	184

Fluency Test

[ ] − [ ] = [ ] (wcpm)

Running Record

Oral Reading Accuracy: Reading Rate:

$$\frac{[\quad] - [\quad]}{[\quad]} \times 100 = [\quad \%]$$ $$\frac{[\quad]}{[\quad]} \times 60 = [\quad] \text{ (wpm)}$$

Rabbit's Tail

Two little long-tailed rabbits sat beside the river. A large turtle was in the water, warming her shell in the sun.

"The grass is greener on the other side," said one rabbit.

"I know how we can get across," said the other. He called out, "Auntie Turtle! I was told your family was bigger than mine, but I do not believe it."

"It's true," she said. She offered to have her whole family float there in the river so the rabbit could count them. Then the rabbit gathered his whole family on the bank of the river so Auntie could count them.

When all the turtles were floating in a line across the river, the rabbits hopped across them to the other side. "Ha!" cried the rabbit. "We fooled you into helping us cross the river!"

The rabbits began nibbling the grass and did not see Auntie Turtle crawling as fast as she could up the bank. She snapped their tails off as punishment for fooling her. And that is why a rabbit now has a fluffy ball where a tail used to be.

Student Name _____ **Date** _____

Camp Dragonfly

Mary and her best friend, Ann, were at Camp Dragonfly. Their parents would drop	14
them off early in the morning and then pick them up after lunch. It was almost the	31
end of July. Today was Friday, the final day of camp. The girls had been discussing	47
the camp's name all month, and they spent most of the swim hour hunting in the	63
weeds at the pond's edge.	68
"There's not a single dragonfly at Camp Dragonfly," Mary complained, swatting	79
at the tall weeds with one hand.	86
"I think there's at least one," Ann said.	94
"You always look on the bright side," Mary said, gazing up directly at the sun.	109
"I always look on the other side."	116
Ann smiled. "Let's describe one, and maybe it will hear us and fly over."	130
"That won't work," Mary said, "but we can try."	139
"Okay," Ann said. "It has long glassy wings."	147
"Its body is skinny like a french fry."	155
"But gray."	157
They gave their dragonfly a sunny personality and named her Jasmine, after the	170
flower, and talked about her until it was time for lunch and the going-away party.	185
"I feel like I really saw Jasmine," Mary said, surprised.	195

Fluency Test

[　　] – [　　] = [　　] (wcpm)

Running Record

Oral Reading Accuracy:

$$\frac{[\quad] - [\quad]}{[\quad]} \times 100 = [\quad]\%$$

Reading Rate:

$$\frac{[\quad]}{[\quad]} \times 60 = [\quad] \text{ (wpm)}$$

Camp Dragonfly

Mary and her best friend, Ann, were at Camp Dragonfly. Their parents would drop them off early in the morning and then pick them up after lunch. It was almost the end of July. Today was Friday, the final day of camp. The girls had been discussing the camp's name all month, and they spent most of the swim hour hunting in the weeds at the pond's edge.

"There's not a single dragonfly at Camp Dragonfly," Mary complained, swatting at the tall weeds with one hand.

"I think there's at least one," Ann said.

"You always look on the bright side," Mary said, gazing up directly at the sun. "I always look on the other side."

Ann smiled. "Let's describe one, and maybe it will hear us and fly over."

"That won't work," Mary said, "but we can try."

"Okay," Ann said. "It has long glassy wings."

"Its body is skinny like a french fry."

"But gray."

They gave their dragonfly a sunny personality and named her Jasmine, after the flower, and talked about her until it was time for lunch and the going-away party.

"I feel like I really saw Jasmine," Mary said, surprised.

Student Name _____ _____ **Date** _____

See Spot Sit

Teaching your dog to sit or to stay is not hard, but it takes practice. Your dog	17
likes to spend time with you. He probably follows you around to see what you are	33
doing. To teach your dog to sit when you tell him to, fill a small bag or cup with	52
treats—small cubes of cheese or hot dog will work—and let him get a sniff of the	70
container. He will pay very close attention to you after he smells these treats!	84
Now stand in front of your dog and look down at his eager face. Show him a	101
treat, holding it in one hand with the tips of your fingers. Lower your hand so it	118
is just above his nose and move it backward so he has to tip his head up to follow	137
its path. Say, "SIT," in a firm and pleasant voice as you do this. He will have to sit	156
in order to stay balanced. As soon as he sits, say, "Good sit!" and move your hand	173
quickly so the treat is held just in front of his mouth. That way he will bend toward	191
the treat and is likely to take it from your hand gently.	203

Fluency Test

[   ] – [   ] = [   ] (wcpm)

Running Record

Oral Reading Accuracy:

$$\frac{[\quad] - [\quad]}{[\quad]} \times 100 = \boxed{\quad \%}$$

Reading Rate:

$$\frac{[\quad]}{[\quad]} \times 60 = \boxed{\quad} \text{ (wpm)}$$

See Spot Sit

Teaching your dog to sit or to stay is not hard, but it takes practice. Your dog likes to spend time with you. He probably follows you around to see what you are doing. To teach your dog to sit when you tell him to, fill a small bag or cup with treats—small cubes of cheese or hot dog will work—and let him get a sniff of the container. He will pay very close attention to you after he smells these treats!

Now stand in front of your dog and look down at his eager face. Show him a treat, holding it in one hand with the tips of your fingers. Lower your hand so it is just above his nose and move it backward so he has to tip his head up to follow its path. Say, "SIT," in a firm and pleasant voice as you do this. He will have to sit in order to stay balanced. As soon as he sits, say, "Good sit!" and move your hand quickly so the treat is held just in front of his mouth. That way he will bend toward the treat and is likely to take it from your hand gently.

Student Name _____ **Date** _____

Why Do You Ask?

"What are you doing?" my little brother Ned asked.	9
"Take a guess," I said. Ned asked too many questions.	19
"Building a fort?"	22
"Yeah," I said and went back to arranging the pine branches, finally adding,	35
"You can help me if you want."	42
That night at dinner, I asked Mom, "Why must we have salad with dinner?"	56
"Take a guess," she said.	61
"In order to get plenty of vegetables?"	68
"If you knew already," she said, "why did you ask?"	78
I gave some thought to the various questions—for example, mine, Ned's,	90
Mom's, and Dad's. What's really being asked, or why it's being asked, can be	104
tricky. Like Ned, people frequently ask questions they know the answer to because	117
they want attention from the person they're asking. When Ned asks what I'm	130
doing, what he's usually asking is whether he can do it with me. My question	145
about salad was different; I wanted to find out if I was right. Mom's question was a	162
slippery one—a deep one without a real answer—so it sent me off to ponder. Dad's	179
questions are typically requests for information. "What are we having for dinner?"	191
he'll ask, or "What grade did you get in math?" One interesting thing about	205
questions is that once they've been asked, we generally feel a need to answer them.	220

Fluency Test

[ ] – [ ] = [ ] (wcpm)

Running Record

Oral Reading Accuracy:

$$\frac{[\quad] - [\quad]}{[\quad]} \times 100 = [\quad] \%$$

Reading Rate:

$$\frac{[\quad]}{[\quad]} \times 60 = [\quad] \text{ (wpm)}$$

Why Do You Ask?

"What are you doing?" my little brother Ned asked.

"Take a guess," I said. Ned asked too many questions.

"Building a fort?"

"Yeah," I said and went back to arranging the pine branches, finally adding, "You can help me if you want."

That night at dinner, I asked Mom, "Why must we have salad with dinner?"

"Take a guess," she said.

"In order to get plenty of vegetables?"

"If you knew already," she said, "why did you ask?"

I gave some thought to the various questions—for example, mine, Ned's, Mom's, and Dad's. What's really being asked, or why it's being asked, can be tricky. Like Ned, people frequently ask questions they know the answer to because they want attention from the person they're asking. When Ned asks what I'm doing, what he's usually asking is whether he can do it with me. My question about salad was different; I wanted to find out if I was right. Mom's question was a slippery one—a deep one without a real answer—so it sent me off to ponder. Dad's questions are typically requests for information. "What are we having for dinner?" he'll ask, or "What grade did you get in math?" One interesting thing about questions is that once they've been asked, we generally feel a need to answer them.

Student Name _____ Date _____

Singing Hoppers

Crickets and grasshoppers both have five eyes, two of which are very large.	13
Their eyes enable them to see to the front, to the side, and to the rear. Two	30
antennae, feelers used for smelling and finding food, grow out of their heads.	43
Crickets live in fields, trees, and houses. They dine on plants and other things,	57
sometimes even clothing. The grasshopper diet consists largely of plants—leaves,	68
flower petals, and seeds—and grasshoppers live wherever plants grow: gardens,	79
fields, and deserts. Grasshoppers are mostly green or brown, a coloring that enables	92
them to blend in with their surroundings.	99
The males of both insects use their body parts to make a "song." Their song is	115
made by rubbing their wings together or scraping a back leg across a wing.	129
Crickets lay their eggs in the ground one at a time. Grasshoppers dig down	143
about an inch and lay as many as a hundred eggs and surround them with foam	159
that hardens into a pod. When a baby grasshopper hatches in the spring, it looks	174
just like an adult but does not have wings. Its hard outer shell cannot grow, so it	191
breaks through and leaves the shell behind. This process is called "molting." The	204
grasshopper's skin hardens into a new shell, and the grasshopper molts again. After	217
each molt, the wings grow bigger. After five or six molts, the grasshopper is ready	232
to fly.	234

Fluency Test

[   ] − [   ] = [   ] (wcpm)

Running Record

Oral Reading Accuracy: Reading Rate:

$$\frac{[\ ] - [\ ]}{[\ ]} \times 100 = [\quad] \%$$
$$\frac{[\ ]}{[\ ]} \times 60 = [\quad] \text{ (wpm)}$$

Singing Hoppers

Crickets and grasshoppers both have five eyes, two of which are very large. Their eyes enable them to see to the front, to the side, and to the rear. Two antennae, feelers used for smelling and finding food, grow out of their heads.

Crickets live in fields, trees, and houses. They dine on plants and other things, sometimes even clothing. The grasshopper diet consists largely of plants—leaves, flower petals, and seeds—and grasshoppers live wherever plants grow: gardens, fields, and deserts. Grasshoppers are mostly green or brown, a coloring that enables them to blend in with their surroundings.

The males of both insects use their body parts to make a "song." Their song is made by rubbing their wings together or scraping a back leg across a wing.

Crickets lay their eggs in the ground one at a time. Grasshoppers dig down about an inch and lay as many as a hundred eggs and surround them with foam that hardens into a pod. When a baby grasshopper hatches in the spring, it looks just like an adult but does not have wings. Its hard outer shell cannot grow, so it breaks through and leaves the shell behind. This process is called "molting." The grasshopper's skin hardens into a new shell, and the grasshopper molts again. After each molt, the wings grow bigger. After five or six molts, the grasshopper is ready to fly.

Student Name _____ Date _____

Talk About Cat Talk

All cats are born already knowing how to purr. Kittens will purr when they	14
are nursing, and a grown-up cat will usually purr when its owner pets it. A cat has	31
more than one purr. A cat can purr a deep rumble, a scratchy whisper, or an uneven	48
clacking sound. The type of purr depends on the mood of the cat. When a cat is	65
falling asleep, it will sometimes give a long purring sigh that goes from clear to	80
muffled. Purring does not necessarily mean a cat is in a happy state of mind—a cat	97
will sometimes purr when it is scared or nervous.	106
Cats also have more than one kind of meow. The one owners hear most often	121
is usually a demand meaning, "I want to be fed," or "I want to go out," or "Pay	139
attention!" Additionally, there is a soft meow that means, "Will you pet me?"	152
Meows that humans do not often hear include a hunting meow and a trilling meow.	167
The trilling meow is almost like a bird's song, and mother cats use it with their	183
kittens.	184
When your cat rubs against your legs or rubs her head and chin on you, she is	201
saying, "You are mine." A cat does this only to a person she trusts. She leaves a	218
scent on you that other cats can smell but people can't. That scent lets all other cats	235
know that you belong to her.	241

Fluency Test

[ ] – [ ] = [ ] (wcpm)

Running Record

Oral Reading Accuracy:

$$\frac{[\quad] - [\quad]}{[\quad]} \times 100 = [\quad\quad] \%$$

Reading Rate:

$$\frac{[\quad]}{[\quad]} \times 60 = [\quad\quad] \text{ (wpm)}$$

Talk About Cat Talk

All cats are born already knowing how to purr. Kittens will purr when they are nursing, and a grown-up cat will usually purr when its owner pets it. A cat has more than one purr. A cat can purr a deep rumble, a scratchy whisper, or an uneven clacking sound. The type of purr depends on the mood of the cat. When a cat is falling asleep, it will sometimes give a long purring sigh that goes from clear to muffled. Purring does not necessarily mean a cat is in a happy state of mind—a cat will sometimes purr when it is scared or nervous.

Cats also have more than one kind of meow. The one owners hear most often is usually a demand meaning, "I want to be fed," or "I want to go out," or "Pay attention!" Additionally, there is a soft meow that means, "Will you pet me?" Meows that humans do not often hear include a hunting meow and a trilling meow. The trilling meow is almost like a bird's song, and mother cats use it with their kittens.

When your cat rubs against your legs or rubs her head and chin on you, she is saying, "You are mine." A cat does this only to a person she trusts. She leaves a scent on you that other cats can smell but people can't. That scent lets all other cats know that you belong to her.

NAME _____ DATE _____

Scott Foresman
Benchmark Test
Unit 1
Living and Learning

Reading STREET

Grade 3

PEARSON

Glenview, Illinois
Boston, Massachusetts
Chandler, Arizona
Upper Saddle River, New Jersey

ISBN-13: 978-0-328-53737-2
ISBN-10:   0-328-53737-3

ISBN-13: 978-0-328-53737-2
ISBN-10:   0-328-53737-3

1 2 3 4 5 6 7 8 9 10 V016 19 18 17 16 15 14 13 12 11 10
CC1

PART 1: COMPREHENSION

Directions
This story is about a family of three bears who find someone in their house.
Read about Baby Bear's reaction. Then do Numbers 1 through 9.

Baby Bear's Story

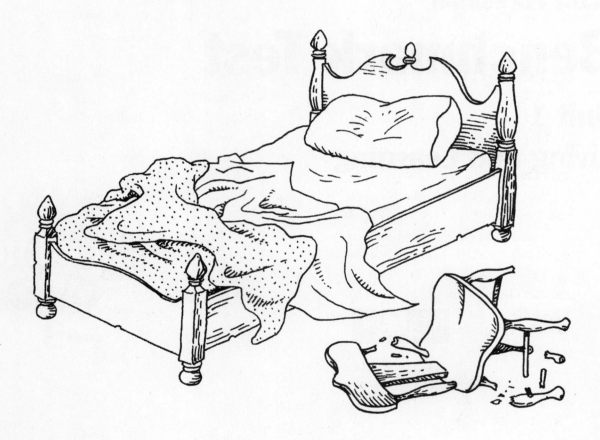

My name is Baby Bear. I live with my parents, Papa Bear and Mama
Bear, in a little house in a big forest. We live simply and happily together. But
yesterday our peaceful lives were upset.

Mama made our breakfast oatmeal as usual. And, as usual, we went for
a walk until the oatmeal was cool enough to eat. Papa picked berries for the
oatmeal. Mama picked flowers for the table. I ran and jumped and played.

When we got back home, the front door was unlocked. "I'm sure that I
locked the door," Mama said.

"Let's move cautiously," said Papa. "There may be someone in the house."

We crept into the house. We could see that someone had been eating our oatmeal. Mama and Papa growled that somebody had nibbled at their bowls. My bowl was completely empty. "Somebody has eaten my oatmeal all up!" I wailed.

"That's okay, Baby Bear," said Mama. "I'll fix you a nice new bowl of oatmeal. We will put berries in it."

I smiled at Mama. Then I went over to sit in my special chair to wait for my oatmeal. That's when I noticed my chair was all broken to pieces. "Somebody has broken my chair!" I cried.

"That's OK, Baby Bear," said Papa. "After breakfast, I'll fix your chair. It will be as good as new."

I smiled at Papa. "I think we should look for who did these things," I said.

"Good thinking, Baby Bear," said my parents. We started searching the house.

I was the one who found her. "Look," I called to my parents. "She's sleeping in my bed."

The three of us gazed down at the sleeping blond girl. She seemed harmless enough.

"She was probably hungry," I whispered. "I'm sure she didn't mean to break my chair. Maybe she would like to play with me when she wakes up."

She must have heard my voice. Her eyelids fluttered open. She looked up and saw the three of us standing over her.

I smiled at her, but that seemed to frighten her. She leaped from the bed and raced out the door. She ran into the woods as fast as she could.

I felt sad because I really did want to play with her. Then Mama reminded me that she was going to make me some breakfast. Papa reminded me that he was going to fix my chair. I gave them each a hug. Then I sat down on the porch to wait for my oatmeal.

1 **What is the setting of this story?**

○ a zoo in the city

○ a school for bears

○ a neighborhood park

○ a house in the woods

GO ON

2 **Who is telling this story?**

○ an unnamed narrator

○ Baby Bear

○ the blond girl

○ Papa Bear

3 **Which of these best describes Baby Bear?**

○ angry

○ silly

○ kind

○ scared

4 **What first made the bears think something was wrong?**

○ The oatmeal was eaten.

○ A chair was broken.

○ The door was unlocked.

○ A girl ran out of the door.

5 **After Baby Bear smiled at her, what did the girl do?**

○ She fixed the chair she had broken.

○ She played with Baby Bear.

○ She made breakfast for the bears.

○ She ran into the woods.

6 **Why did Baby Bear hug his parents?**

○ He was glad about what they promised to do.

○ He was happy that everybody was safe.

○ He wanted them to protect him from the girl.

○ He felt sad and lonely.

7 What was the last thing Baby Bear did in the story?

○ He ate his oatmeal.

○ He sat on the porch.

○ He found the girl sleeping.

○ He watched the girl run away.

8 How did Baby Bear feel when he saw the girl?

○ He was angry at her for breaking his chair.

○ He liked her and wanted to play with her.

○ He thought she should live with his family.

○ He was afraid that she would hurt him.

9 What lesson did the girl probably learn in this story?

○ You should stay out of strange places.

○ Animals need to lock their doors.

○ It is important to eat all the food on your plate.

○ Bears are dangerous animals.

GO ON

Directions

Write your answer to Question A on the lines below. Base your answer on "Baby Bear's Story."

A Think about how the girl felt when she woke up and saw the bears. How would you have felt? What would you have done? Explain why.

_____

_____

_____

_____

_____

_____

_____

_____

_____

Directions

Read this story about a rich man and a poor man. Then do Numbers 10 through 18.

Money Means Worries

A rich merchant named Chen had all the money he needed. He lived in perfect comfort. His food was rich, his bed was soft, and his clothing was beautiful.

A poor potter named Li lived next door. He did not have much money. He ate simple food, he slept on the floor, and he wore old, plain clothes. His only treasure was a golden canary that lived in a wooden cage.

The merchant worked day and night. He hunched over his account books, adding and subtracting. He yelled at his clerks and made them work as hard as he did. He rarely stopped working to eat a real meal. He ate at his desk and hardly noticed the delicious food. Late at night, the tired man went to bed, but he was unable to sleep. Thinking about money, he tossed and turned in his soft bed.

GO ON

His neighbor spent the day making pots from clay. At the end of the day, Li sat in his garden and enjoyed a simple supper. Then he brought his canary outside. Li played his flute while the canary sang. At night, Li slept soundly on his floor.

For years, the music from the garden had disturbed the merchant. It made him angry. One sleepless night, he came up with a plan to make the music stop.

The next afternoon, he visited his neighbor. He held out a sack of gold coins and gave it to Li. Chen said, "You have been a good neighbor for many years. Here is a gift for you."

Li thanked Chen. Then he sat in his garden, thinking about the money. Should he hide it? Should he spend it? The poor canary cried for its owner, but Li was lost in his thoughts. He forgot about his supper. He forgot about his flute. He thought all night long.

Chen grinned happily at the success of his plan. He knew that having money would destroy Li's simple pleasures.

Li made no pots the next day. He did not eat or play the flute. He just worried about the money all day. He worried throughout the long, sleepless night.

The next morning, his canary took pity on him. "Money means worries," she sang. "Give it back. Give it back."

Li heard the canary's song. He remembered how happy he had been before the money arrived. He picked up the bag of coins and went next door.

10 **How did the merchant spend his time?**
- ◯   working and thinking about money
- ◯   enjoying the pleasures of life
- ◯   studying books and creating music
- ◯   eating fine food with his friends

11 **Why was Chen angry?**
- ◯   His clerks were cheating him.
- ◯   Li's happiness disturbed him.
- ◯   His neighbors were richer than he was.
- ◯   Li made beautiful pots while he only made money.

12 **Which of these story events happened first?**

○ Li's canary spoke to him.

○ Li couldn't sleep.

○ Li thought about money.

○ Li was given a bag of coins.

13 **Which of these best describes Chen?**

○ busy and happy

○ kind and gentle

○ curious and amused

○ worried and angry

14 **What did Li probably do with the bag of coins?**

○ He buried it in a safe place.

○ He gave it back to Chen.

○ He hired people to help him make pots.

○ He bought new clothes and a soft bed.

15 **What happened just after Li got the gold coins?**

○ He enjoyed a simple supper in his garden.

○ He played his flute while his canary sang.

○ He worried about what to do with the money.

○ He made a beautiful pot from clay.

16 **What happened after Li forgot to play his flute?**

○ Chen felt happy.

○ Li ate his supper.

○ Chen gave Li money.

○ Li felt surprised.

GO ON

17 **What lesson did Li learn in this story?**

   ○   Nature is beautiful.

   ○   People should save their money.

   ○   Money does not buy happiness.

   ○   It is important to be a good neighbor.

18 **What would be another good title for this story?**

   ○   "The Magic Canary"

   ○   "A Mean Neighbor"

   ○   "Rich with Happiness"

   ○   "Music and Money"

Directions

Write your answer to Question B on the lines below. Base your answer on the two stories you have read.

B Think about "Baby Bear's Story" and "Money Means Worries." Which story seems most like something that could happen in real life? Explain your thinking.

PART 2: VOCABULARY

Directions
Fill in the circle beside your answer choice for Numbers 19 through 24.

19 Read the following sentence:

Let's move <u>cautiously</u>.

What does <u>cautiously</u> mean?
- ○ without caution
- ○ instead of caution
- ○ in a cautious way
- ○ too cautious

20 Read the following sentence:

She seemed <u>harmless</u> enough.

What does <u>harmless</u> mean?
- ○ full of harm
- ○ in a way that does harm
- ○ the state of harm
- ○ without harm

21 Which word is a compound word?
- ○ sleeping
- ○ eyelids
- ○ frighten
- ○ reminded

22 Which meaning of the homonym <u>plain</u> is used in the following sentence?

He wore old, <u>plain</u> clothes.

- ○ flat
- ○ pure
- ○ clear
- ○ simple

23 If you wanted to look up the word <u>treasure</u> in the dictionary, between which two words would <u>treasure</u> appear alphabetically?

- ○ *tray* and *treat*
- ○ *tree* and *tricky*
- ○ *trash* and *treason*
- ○ *trend* and *trip*

24 When the bears got home, the door was <u>unlocked</u>.

What does <u>unlocked</u> mean?

- ○ not locked
- ○ double-locked
- ○ well locked
- ○ locked again

PART 3: PHONICS

Directions
Fill in the circle beside your answer choice for Numbers 25 through 34.

25 Li sat in his garden and enjoyed a simple <u>supper</u>.

Which word has the same middle sound as the <u>pp</u> in <u>supper</u>?

- ○ open
- ○ nap
- ○ rabbit
- ○ pilot

26 Li played his flute while the <u>canary</u> sang.

What is the plural form of the word <u>canary</u>?

- ○ canarys
- ○ canaries
- ○ canareys
- ○ canary's

27 Baby Bear said, "I <u>live</u> with my parents."

What is the past tense of the word <u>live</u>?

- ○ lives
- ○ liveed
- ○ lived
- ○ living

28 Baby Bear sat down on the porch to <u>wait</u> for his oatmeal.

Which word has the same sound as the <u>ai</u> in <u>wait</u>?

- ○ sad
- ○ hand
- ○ dark
- ○ face

29 Baby Bear was the one who <u>found</u> her.

Which word has the same sound as the <u>ou</u> in <u>found</u>?

○ cow

○ front

○ through

○ close

30 Chen came <u>up</u> with a plan.

Which word has the same vowel sound as <u>up</u>?

○ turned

○ must

○ flute

○ music

31 Which of these words is spelled correctly?

○ porches

○ partys

○ cherrys

○ foxs

32 Baby Bear felt <u>sad</u> when the girl ran away.

Which word means <u>more sad</u>?

○ sadly

○ saddest

○ sadness

○ sadder

GO ON

33 Someone has been <u>eating</u> our oatmeal.

Which word has the same sound as the <u>ea</u> in <u>eating</u>?

○ search

○ break

○ three

○ been

34 He held out a sack of gold <u>coins</u> and gave it to Li.

Which word has the same sound as the <u>oi</u> in <u>coins</u>?

○ toys

○ scouts

○ grow

○ whole

PART 4: WRITING CONVENTIONS

*D*irections
Fill in the circle beside your answer choice for Numbers 35 through 40.

35 **Which sentence has the correct punctuation?**

- ○ Do you know his name.
- ○ Sacramento is the capital of California,
- ○ Don't plant the seeds too deep?
- ○ Are you ready?

36 **Choose the words that best complete this sentence.**

My best friend Emily _____.

- ○ behind me in class
- ○ every day after school
- ○ has a new pet hamster
- ○ eating a ham sandwich

37 **What is the subject of the sentence below?**

Every morning Sam takes the bus to school.

- ○ Every morning
- ○ Sam
- ○ takes
- ○ the bus to school

38 **Which sentence should have a question mark at the end?**

- ○ Don't run in the hallway
- ○ How happy everyone is
- ○ The weather is very nice
- ○ What time is it

GO ON

39 **Which sentence is a command?**

○ Put away your books.

○ Henry read his report to the class.

○ The painting is amazing!

○ There is someone at the door.

40 **Which sentence is a compound sentence?**

○ My brother likes swimming, but I like hiking.

○ Miss Johnson's gym class is playing a new game today.

○ There is a very large maple tree next to their house.

○ I wrote a letter to my aunt and uncle.

PART 5: WRITING

PROMPT

"Baby Bear's Story" is written as a personal narrative. In it, he tells an interesting story of something that happened to him one day. Think about a day when something interesting happened in your life. Tell the story of what happened that day.

CHECKLIST FOR WRITERS

_____ Did I think about a day when something interesting happened to me?

_____ Did I take notes about that day before I started writing?

_____ Did I tell my story in the order in which it happened?

_____ Did I use words and details that clearly express my ideas?

_____ Do my sentences make sense?

_____ Did I check my sentences for proper grammar and punctuation?

_____ Did I check my spelling?

_____ Did I make sure my paper is the way I want readers to read it?

Scott Foresman
Benchmark Test
Unit 2
Smart Solutions

PEARSON

Glenview, Illinois
Boston, Massachusetts
Chandler, Arizona
Upper Saddle River, New Jersey

Grade 3

Copyright © Pearson Education, Inc., or its affiliates. All Rights Reserved.
Printed in the United States of America. This publication is protected by copyright,
and permission should be obtained from the publisher prior to any prohibited
reproduction, storage in a retrieval system, or transmission in any form or by any
means, electronic, mechanical, photocopying, recording, or likewise. The publisher
hereby grants permission to reproduce these pages, in part or in whole, for classroom
use only, the number not to exceed the number of students in each class. Notice of
copyright must appear on all copies. For information regarding permissions, write to
Pearson Curriculum Group Rights & Permissions, One Lake Street, Upper Saddle River,
New Jersey 07458.

Pearson, Scott Foresman, and Pearson Scott Foresman are trademarks, in the U.S.
and/or other countries, of Pearson Education, Inc., or its affiliates.

ISBN-13: 978-0-328-53738-9
ISBN-10:   0-328-53738-1

1 2 3 4 5 6 7 8 9 10 V016 19 18 17 16 15 14 13 12 11 10
CC1

ISBN-13: 978-0-328-53738-9
ISBN-10:   0-328-53738-1

PART 1: COMPREHENSION

Directions

Read about an ant and a dove who help each other. Then answer Numbers 1 through 9.

The Ant and the Dove

One day an ant was out for a morning stroll in his neighborhood park. Feeling a little thirsty, he climbed up on the rim of a fountain and leaned toward the water to get a drink. PLOP! SPLASH! He tumbled into the water. Sadly, ants can't swim. He struggled in the water, afraid that he might drown.

"Help!" he cried, as loudly as he could.

At that very minute, a dove was flying over the fountain and heard the ant's faint cry for help. She looked down to find the source of the sound. She saw the ant struggling in the water. She knew that ants can't swim.

"How can I help him?" she asked herself. "I can't fly down and pick him up. I might crush him."

The dove thought hard for a minute. Then she flew over to a big oak tree and tore off a large leaf. Holding the leaf in her beak, she flew back to the fountain and dropped the leaf in the water, close to the ant.

The ant looked puzzled until he realized that help had arrived. He quickly climbed up on the leaf and sailed safely to the edge of the fountain. Waving his thanks to the dove, he climbed down to the ground.

The next morning the ant was back in the park. It was a lovely day for a walk. The ant was happily humming his favorite song.

All of a sudden, the ant saw the dove. She was walking along a path, looking for food. The ant started to shout hello to his friend. Then he noticed a man sneaking up on the dove. The man had a net in his hand. The ant guessed that the man wanted to capture the dove in the net.

"How can I help the dove?" the ant thought. "She saved me, and now it's my turn to save her. But how can one little ant stop a big man?"

The ant thought hard for a minute. Then he scurried over to the man's feet and climbed up the man's leg. When the ant got to bare skin, he bit the man as hard as he could.

"Ouch!" yelled the man, and he dropped the net. Alerted by the noise, the dove flew away. As she went, she waved her thanks to the ant.

Moral: One good turn deserves another.

1 **Which of these best describes the dove?**

- ○ dirty and hungry
- ○ neat and eager
- ○ tricky and mean
- ○ clever and kind

2 **Which part of the setting is most important to the events of the story?**

- ○ the fountain
- ○ the ground
- ○ the tree
- ○ the sun

3 **Which of these best describes the ant?**

- ○ big and strong
- ○ smart and caring
- ○ curious and puzzled
- ○ silly and fun

4 How were the ant and the dove alike?

○ They were good at solving problems.

○ They enjoyed swimming and other sports.

○ They were proud of their good looks.

○ They were quiet and patient.

5 In the selection, one way that the ant and the dove were different was

○ the dove could walk, but the ant could not.

○ the ant could talk, but the dove could not.

○ the dove could fly, but the ant could not.

○ the dove could swim, but the ant could not.

6 Why did the ant bite the man?

○ to get the food he needed

○ to stop the man from crushing the ant

○ to show the dove how brave he was

○ to repay the dove for helping the ant

7 What happened first in the story?

○ The man tried to catch the dove.

○ The ant fell into the water.

○ The dove flew to the tree.

○ The ant bit the man.

8   **What is the theme of this selection?**

○   Don't judge others by the way they look.

○   Only say nice things about others.

○   Treat others as you would like to be treated.

○   Don't attack others even if they attack you.

9   **One way that the ant and the dove were the same was that both**

○   liked to play in the trees.

○   acted without thinking.

○   were willing to help others.

○   tried to hurt people in the park.

A **This story teaches a lesson. What is the lesson? How do the ant's actions show that lesson?**

_____

_____

_____

_____

_____

_____

_____

_____

_____

Directions
The game of basketball was invented to solve a problem. Read about this invention. Then answer Numbers 10 through 18.

James Naismith's Problem

James Naismith was a gym teacher with a problem. He had a class of eighteen young men who were hard to work with. They thought the usual gym exercises were boring. They hated gym class, and so they misbehaved. Naismith's boss told him to invent a new game for the students.

Naismith was a very young teacher. The year before, he had been a student in the same school. It was December of 1891. The Massachusetts winter was cold, so the students could not play outside. He would have to invent an indoor sport. The game needed to be easy to learn so that he could teach it to his class quickly. It had to be active and interesting. Above all, it had to be safe—for both the students and the gym.

GO ON

His boss, Dr. Luther Gulik, had given him fourteen days to come up with an idea that worked. Naismith first tried to bring outdoor games, such as soccer and football, inside. These games weren't safe, though. Players got hurt on the hard floors. These games damaged the gym walls and floors. Naismith tried lacrosse, but that led to more injuries.

Naismith felt discouraged. Then he had the idea of looking at popular team games to see what they shared. He realized that all the games had a ball. That meant a ball should be part of his new game. He decided to use a soccer ball. To keep players from getting hurt, he decided that the players should not tackle each other. He decided to put a goal at each end of the gym. Two old peach baskets were used as goals. He placed these goals above the players' heads. This meant that the players would throw the ball up in the air toward the goal.

Naismith sat at his desk and wrote thirteen rules for his new game. When the students came in, Naismith showed them the rules and explained the game. The class formed two teams, each with nine players. The young men liked the game as soon as they started playing it. When the class was over, Naismith went to Dr. Gulik's office. He reported that his problem had been solved. The solution was the new game he called "basket ball."

10 **The main idea of this selection is that James Naismith**

- ○ had students who were hard to work with.
- ○ invented basketball to solve a problem.
- ○ was a gym teacher in Massachusetts.
- ○ didn't want his students to get hurt in the gym.

11 **What was Naismith's problem in this selection?**

- ○ He needed a new game to keep his students under control.
- ○ His boss was going to fire him if he couldn't control his class.
- ○ He didn't like the cold winter weather.
- ○ He would rather have been a student than a teacher.

12 **The fourth paragraph is mostly about**

- ○ which outdoor games used a ball.
- ○ how Naismith came up with a new game.
- ○ why Naismith needed to invent a new game.
- ○ how Naismith felt about his job.

13 **What problem did Naismith find with playing lacrosse indoors?**

○   The students didn't like it.

○   Gym windows got broken.

○   The equipment was too expensive.

○   The players got hurt.

14 **How were *all* the sports James Naismith studied alike?**

○   They used a ball.

○   They were boring to his students.

○   They were played only in the winter.

○   They had goals above the players' heads.

15 **Naismith did not allow tackling in his new game because**

○   Dr. Gulik was against tackling.

○   most other games didn't have tackling.

○   he didn't want players to get hurt.

○   his students didn't like rough games.

16 **What did Naismith do first to solve his problem?**

○   He studied how other games were played.

○   He tried soccer and football indoors.

○   He talked to his students.

○   He wrote the rules for a new game.

17 **How did Naismith probably feel about his invention after his class played their first game?**

○ surprised that the rules didn't work

○ a little discouraged

○ determined to do better

○ very pleased

18 **What is the author's purpose in writing this selection?**

○ to entertain the reader with a funny basketball story

○ to persuade the reader to try playing basketball

○ to tell the reader about how basketball began

○ to teach the reader how to play basketball

Directions

Write your answer to Question B on the lines below. Base your answer on the two selections you have read.

B In what way were the ant and the dove like James Naismith? Use details from both selections to support your answer.

PART 2: VOCABULARY

*D*irections
Fill in the circle beside your answer choice for Numbers 19 through 24.

19 The ant was out for a morning <u>stroll</u> in his neighborhood park.

What is a synonym for <u>stroll</u>?

- ○ walk
- ○ swim
- ○ meal
- ○ adventure

20 The ant leaned toward the water and <u>tumbled</u> into the fountain.

What is a synonym for <u>tumbled</u>?

- ○ flew
- ○ fell
- ○ looked
- ○ jumped

21 The dove heard the ant's <u>faint</u> cry for help.

What is an antonym for <u>faint</u>?

- ○ hopeful
- ○ happy
- ○ worried
- ○ loud

22 Naismith needed to <u>invent</u> a new game.

What is a synonym for <u>invent</u>?

- ○ share
- ○ buy
- ○ make
- ○ play

23 Which pair of words from "James Naismith's Problem" are antonyms?

○ safe—popular

○ boring—interesting

○ goal—basket

○ wrote—explained

24 Naismith went to Dr. Gulik's office and <u>reported</u> that his problem had been solved. Which word means the same as <u>reported</u>?

○ hoped

○ lied

○ wrote

○ stated

PART 3: PHONICS

*D*irections
Fill in the circle beside your answer choice for Numbers 25 through 34.

25 How is the word <u>student</u> correctly divided into syllables?

○ stude / nt

○ stu / dent

○ st / udent

○ stud / ent

26 Which word is a compound word?

○ teacher

○ popular

○ soccer

○ outdoor

27 Which word is broken into syllables correctly?

○ rea / lized

○ flo / ors

○ dam / aged

○ wint / er

28 How is the word <u>maple</u> correctly divided into syllables?

○ ma / ple

○ m / aple

○ map / le

○ mapl / e

29 Which word begins with the same sound as the word <u>phone</u>?

○ plop

○ holding

○ fountain

○ thanks

30 Which word has the same sounds as the <u>str</u> in <u>struggled</u>?

   ◯   started

   ◯   restring

   ◯   interesting

   ◯   sorting

31 Which word is a compound word?

   ◯   football

   ◯   active

   ◯   misbehaved

   ◯   discouraged

32 How is the word <u>second</u> correctly divided into syllables?

   ◯   se / cond

   ◯   seco / nd

   ◯   sec / ond

   ◯   se / co / nd

33 Which word has the same sounds as the <u>spl</u> in <u>splash</u>?

   ◯   spool

   ◯   simple

   ◯   spill

   ◯   splendid

34 Which word has the same sound as the <u>sh</u> in <u>crush</u>?

   ◯   washing

   ◯   which

   ◯   school

   ◯   patch

PART 4: WRITING CONVENTIONS

Directions
Fill in the circle beside your answer choice for Numbers 35 through 40.

35 **Which word can be used as a plural noun?**
- ○ deer
- ○ horse
- ○ mosquito
- ○ robin

36 **In "The Ant and the Dove," the man had a net.**

What is the correct way to speak about the net?
- ○ the mans' net
- ○ the men's net
- ○ the man's net
- ○ the mans net

37 **Naismith had eighteen students in his class.**

What is the correct way to speak about the behavior of all the students?
- ○ the studentes' behavior
- ○ the students behavior
- ○ the student's behavior
- ○ the students' behavior

38 **Which word is a proper noun?**
- ○ lacrosse
- ○ rules
- ○ December
- ○ solution

39 Which word correctly completes the sentence?

In the story, the ant saved the _____ life.

○ doves

○ dove's

○ doves'

○ doves'es

40 Which word correctly completes the sentence?

The basket was ten _____ above the floor.

○ feet

○ foot

○ feets

○ foots

PART 5: WRITING

PROMPT

James Naismith wrote thirteen rules to explain how to play basketball. Think about something you know how to do. It could be a sport or game you play. It could be a way to cook something or make something with your hands. Write a paragraph that tells someone else how to do this thing.

CHECKLIST FOR WRITERS

_____ Did I think about something I know how to do?

_____ Did I list all the steps or rules for doing it?

_____ Did I organize my paragraph in a logical way?

_____ Did I use words and details that clearly express my ideas?

_____ Do my sentences make sense?

_____ Did I check my sentences for proper grammar and punctuation?

_____ Did I check my spelling?

_____ Did I make sure my paper is the way I want readers to read it?

NAME _____ DATE _____

Scott Foresman
Benchmark Test
Unit 3
People and Nature

PEARSON

Glenview, Illinois
Boston, Massachusetts
Chandler, Arizona
Upper Saddle River, New Jersey

ISBN-13: 978-0-328-53739-6
ISBN-10:   0-328-53739-X
1 2 3 4 5 6 7 8 9 10 V016 19 18 17 16 15 14 13 12 11 10
CC1

ISBN-13: 978-0-328-53739-6
ISBN-10:   0-328-53739-X

90000>

EAN

9 780328 537396

Directions
Read this story about a dog named Fred. Then do Numbers 1 through 9.

Thinking Like Fred

Our dog Fred is a very big, highly intelligent dog. Let me tell you a story that proves how smart he is.

Fred joined our family when he was ten weeks old. To help us understand him, we purchased a dog book called *Think Like a Dog*.

We live in the country, so the country is the only environment Fred has ever known. Fred loves adventures and often accompanies us when we go out. He goes shopping with us, and our friends welcome his visits. He has gone camping, swimming, and hiking.

Until last week, however, Fred had never gone to the city. Last week we went to visit my grandmother, who lives on the twentieth floor of a big apartment building.

As we drove into the downtown area, Fred happily gazed at all the new sights. He was completely unafraid.

We arrived at my grandmother's building and went in. We got on the elevator, and Fred seemed perfectly happy to get on too. I pressed the button marked "20," and up we went. When we got off, we noticed that Fred was trembling a little. He looked all around and yawned. Our dog book says that yawning means a dog is thinking about something, and its brain is asking for more oxygen.

When we were in my grandmother's apartment, Fred kept looking out the window. He kept yawning and yawning. Everybody else was having a good time, but Fred seemed upset. He wasn't his usual happy self.

Finally, it was time to go home. We walked out to the elevator and pressed the call button. Fred was shaking as the elevator door opened. We tried to get on the elevator with Fred, but it was impossible. He wouldn't budge. He just looked at the elevator compartment and shook. We tried to reason with him, but it made no difference.

Then I remembered what the dog book said. "Dogs try to make sense of the world. If your dog does something strange, put yourself inside your dog's head. Think like a dog."

So I put myself in Fred's place, and I understood why he was so upset about the elevator. He had walked into a little room, the room had moved, and then he had ended up in a totally different place. He'd never experienced anything like that before. It was clear he didn't plan to experience it ever again.

As we walked down twenty flights of stairs, I kept thinking how smart Fred was.

1 **The author wrote this selection to**
- ○ give information about training dogs.
- ○ persuade the reader to get a dog.
- ○ express feelings about all dogs.
- ○ entertain the reader with a story about a dog.

2 **You can tell that the narrator**
- ○ thinks Fred should live in the city.
- ○ tries hard to understand Fred.
- ○ enjoys climbing stairs for exercise.
- ○ has no sense of humor.

3 Why did the author include the details about Fred's adventures in the country?

○ to prove that Fred was afraid to try new things

○ to show that Fred was usually a happy dog

○ to tell about how Fred came to live with the narrator

○ to explain how Fred learned to swim

4 Fred was yawning in the apartment because

○ he was bored.

○ nobody paid attention to him.

○ the trip had been tiring.

○ he was thinking.

5 Which of these events happened last?

○ Fred refused to get on the elevator.

○ Fred rode the elevator up to the apartment.

○ Fred kept looking out the window.

○ Fred began yawning.

6 The narrator thought that Fred

○ was afraid of small rooms.

○ didn't want to go back to the country.

○ couldn't understand how the elevator worked.

○ didn't like the sound the elevator made.

7 From his behavior in the selection, you can tell that Fred is a dog that

○ likes to make sense of things.

○ will do anything for food.

○ is afraid to be left home alone.

○ barks to get people's attention.

8 In the selection, the author compares Fred's behavior
- ○ before and after he moved to the country.
- ○ before and after his first elevator ride.
- ○ before and after he went camping.
- ○ before and after he walked down the stairs.

9 Which event was most important to the plot of the story?
- ○ Fred joined the narrator's family at ten weeks old.
- ○ The narrator pressed the elevator's call button.
- ○ Fred would not get back on the elevator.
- ○ The narrator tried to reason with the dog.

GO ON

Directions

Write your answer to Question A on the lines below. Base your answer on "Thinking Like Fred."

A   In this selection, the narrator tells us his dog is smart. What do you know about dogs that supports the idea that dogs are smart?

_____

_____

_____

_____

_____

_____

_____

_____

Directions
Read the selection to learn about dogs that help people. Then do Numbers 10 through 18.

Service Dogs

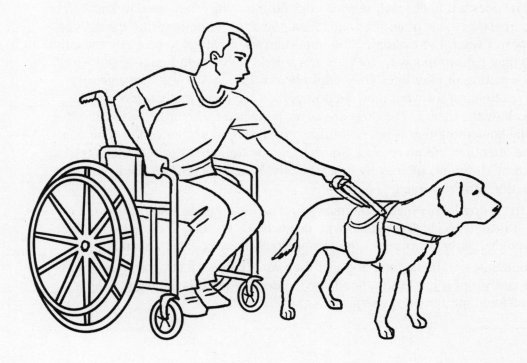

Some people cannot hear, some cannot walk, and some cannot use their arms or hands. Dogs can be trained to help these people. Such canines are known as "service dogs" because they serve people.

A dog that is trained to work with a person who is hearing-impaired listens for certain sounds. The dog lets the person know when the phone or doorbell rings, when the alarm clock goes off, and when the smoke alarm sounds. When the dog hears these noises, it touches its owner, letting the person know what is happening.

Dogs can open doors for people who cannot move without help. These service dogs can also turn lights on and off. They can pick up things that the person drops, like keys or papers or cell phones. They can also bring a wheelchair to the person, and they can even help the person get into the wheelchair!

Many of the groups that train dogs to help people use only rescue dogs, dogs that have been saved from some other situation. These dogs come from animal shelters or from rescue groups. Because of this, the dogs get a home and a special job at the same time.

How does a trainer teach service dogs all the things they need to know? The trainer rewards the actions she wants from the dogs while ignoring the actions she doesn't want. For example, it is important for the dogs to be quiet and calm. When they behave this way, they are rewarded. They might be rewarded with food or petting or playtime. They might be rewarded with praise. By getting positive attention for what they are doing, they are more likely to do it again. This is how they learn. The dogs are never punished for their behavior. If a dog is doing something that is not helpful, the trainer ignores that action. The dog gets no attention and no reward. Sometimes, the trainer will direct the dog to do something different, such as lie down quietly. When the dog succeeds with this new action, it is rewarded.

After a dog learns many commands and actions that will help someone in need, it is matched with a person who needs help. The dog and the person then go through classes, learning even more lessons. They become a team.

Sometimes, trainers get a dog that they cannot use. The dog may be smart and friendly, but it just isn't a good service dog. When this happens, people are allowed to adopt these dogs as pets.

10   **What does a service dog do when there is a noise?**
O   The dog touches its owner.
O   The dog barks loudly.
O   The dog walks to the door.
O   The dog rings a bell.

11   **In this selection, the author compares**
O   how service dogs are trained and how pet dogs are trained.
O   what service dogs do for people who are hearing-impaired and for people who cannot walk.
O   how dogs from shelters behave and how trained dogs behave.
O   the foods trainers use for rewards and the foods service dogs eat every day.

12 **You can tell that a trainer needs to be**

- ○ funny.
- ○ quiet.
- ○ patient.
- ○ angry.

13 **What happens when the trainer gives a dog a reward for doing something?**

- ○ The dog is rescued from a shelter.
- ○ The dog becomes a service dog.
- ○ The dog ignores the trainer.
- ○ The dog will do it again.

14 **Why does the person who needs help go to classes with the dog?**

- ○ so the dog can be adopted as a pet
- ○ so the person can learn about animal shelters
- ○ so the dog can decide if it likes the person
- ○ so the person and the dog can learn to work together

15 **What is the most likely reason the author wrote this selection?**

- ○ to give facts about dogs that help people
- ○ to persuade the reader to get a service dog
- ○ to entertain the reader with a sad story of a dog
- ○ to express feelings about a certain service dog

16 **What would be another good title for this selection?**

- ○ "Police Dogs"
- ○ "People Who Work with Dogs"
- ○ "Training Your Pet Dog "
- ○ "Working Dogs"

17 How does a person who is paired up with a good service dog probably feel?

○ beautiful

○ thankful

○ nervous

○ angry

18 From the trainers' use of shelter dogs, you can tell that

○ they know shelter dogs always make good service dogs.

○ they need dogs that are all the same color.

○ they care about helping animals as well as people.

○ they like to use only a certain size of dog for service dogs.

Directions

Write your answer to Question B on the lines below. Base your answer on the two selections you have read.

B Do you think the narrator in "Thinking Like Fred" would be interested in reading "Service Dogs"? Tell why or why not.

WRITING ACROSS TEXTS

_____

_____

_____

_____

_____

_____

_____

_____

_____

PART 2: VOCABULARY

Directions
Fill in the circle beside your answer choice for Numbers 19 through 24.

19 What does the word <u>helpful</u> mean?

   ○ needing help

   ○ help again

   ○ not able to help

   ○ helping

20 Which word is a compound word?

   ○ impossible

   ○ apartment

   ○ environment

   ○ grandmother

21 You want to find the definition of <u>canine</u> in a dictionary. Between which two words would <u>canine</u> appear alphabetically?

   ○ candy—cannon

   ○ camel—can

   ○ canary—candle

   ○ carpet—carry

22 A dog-training book uses a number of words such as <u>command</u> and <u>ignore</u> in a special way. To find out what these words mean in the book, you can look in the book's

   ○ charts.

   ○ index.

   ○ glossary.

   ○ table of contents.

23 Which word correctly completes this sentence?

Dogs can be trained to help people who cannot _____ by listening for certain noises.

- ○ hire
- ○ hair
- ○ hear
- ○ here

24 Which meaning of the word <u>through</u> is used in the following sentence?

The dog and the person then go <u>through</u> more classes.

- ○ in one side and out the other side of
- ○ in the middle of
- ○ from the beginning to the end of
- ○ because of

PART 3: PHONICS

*D*irections
Fill in the circle beside your answer choice for Numbers 25 through 34.

25 Which of the following is another correct way to write <u>did not</u>?
- ○ did'nt
- ○ did'not
- ○ didn't
- ○ don't

26 What does the word <u>rewrite</u> mean?
- ○ write under
- ○ write again
- ○ write before
- ○ write after

27 Fred lives in the <u>country</u>. Which word has the same sound as the <u>c</u> in <u>country</u>?
- ○ city
- ○ trace
- ○ changes
- ○ kept

28 Fred is a very big, <u>highly</u> intelligent dog. What is the base word of <u>highly</u>?
- ○ high
- ○ hi
- ○ ighly
- ○ ly

29 Which word has the same beginning sound as the <u>kn</u> in <u>kneel</u>?
- ○ castle
- ○ nation
- ○ kingdom
- ○ kennel

30 Read the following sentence:

He'd never experienced anything like that before.

Which two words make up the contraction **He'd**?

○ He will

○ He should

○ He is

○ He had

31 Read the following sentence:

He wasn't his usual happy self.

Which of the following means the opposite of **usual**?

○ unusual

○ reusual

○ misusual

○ disusual

32 Read the following sentence:

Our dog book says that yawning means a dog is thinking about something, and its brain is asking for more **oxygen**.

Which word has the same sound as the **g** in **oxygen**?

○ struggle

○ dogs

○ anger

○ intelligent

33 What is the base word of **happily**?

○ happi

○ ly

○ happy

○ hap

34 Read the following sentence:

A dog that is trained to work with a hearing-impaired person <u>listens</u> for certain sounds.

Which word has the same sound as the <u>st</u> in <u>listens</u>?

○ cars

○ sand

○ moves

○ watches

PART 4: WRITING CONVENTIONS

Directions
Fill in the circle beside your answer choice for Numbers 35 through 40.

35 Cows _____ grass.
- ○ eat
- ○ eats
- ○ eating
- ○ be eating

36 His name _____ Carl.
- ○ be
- ○ is
- ○ are
- ○ were

37 My sister and I _____ twins.
- ○ am
- ○ is
- ○ are
- ○ was

38 Yesterday I _____ to the beach.
- ○ go
- ○ done gone
- ○ went
- ○ goed

GO ON

39 Last week we _____ with our cousins.
- ○ will play
- ○ played
- ○ play
- ○ are playing

40 Next year we _____ in fourth grade.
- ○ were
- ○ was
- ○ have been
- ○ will be

18

PART 5: WRITING

PROMPT

"Service Dogs" tells about dogs that help people with special needs. The people the dogs work with are alike and different in many ways. Think of two people you know or know about. These people can be famous people, fictional characters, or ordinary people. Write about the ways the two people are alike and the ways they are different.

CHECKLIST FOR WRITERS

_____ Did I think about two people I know or know about?

_____ Did I take notes about each person before I started writing?

_____ Did I tell how these people are alike?

_____ Did I tell how these people are different?

_____ Did I use words and details that clearly express my ideas?

_____ Do my sentences make sense?

_____ Did I check my sentences for proper grammar and punctuation?

_____ Did I check my spelling?

_____ Did I make sure my paper is the way I want readers to read it?

NAME _____ DATE _____

Scott Foresman
Benchmark Test
Unit 4
One of a Kind

Glenview, Illinois
Boston, Massachusetts
Chandler, Arizona
Upper Saddle River, New Jersey

ISBN-13: 978-0-328-53740-2
ISBN-10:   0-328-53740-3

1 2 3 4 5 6 7 8 9 10 V016 19 18 17 16 15 14 13 12 11 10
CC1

ISBN-13: 978-0-328-53740-2
ISBN-10:   0-328-53740-3

PART 1: COMPREHENSION

Directions

Mixing art and cars can be fun and amusing. Read about how some cars have been transformed into works of art. Then do Numbers 1 through 9.

Art Cars

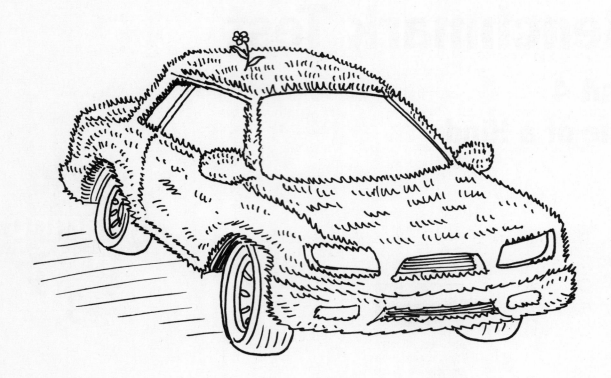

Have you ever seen a car covered with fake fur or one covered with moss? How about a car all wrapped up in aluminum? Imagine a car with mirrors glued to every surface. What about one that has been hand-painted in a loud red plaid? Does that sound impossible? You could not be more wrong. All of these cars exist. They are art cars.

What is an art car? An art car is a regular car that is turned into a work of art by its owner. People who make art cars can get pretty crazy. One car, called "Cootie," has plastic and rubber spiders, ants, flies, grasshoppers, and other bugs stuck all over it. Another car, the Fruitmobile, is a fruit salad on wheels. It is covered with all types of fake fruit.

Art cars have become more and more popular. There are art car parades in many cities now. The oldest one is in Houston, Texas. It began in 1986 with eleven cars. About 1,000 people came to watch. Now the event has more than two hundred unusual art cars, and more than 100,000 people come to see them. It's fun to see how far people will go to outdo each other to have a car totally unlike any other.

No one who has been to an art car parade will think of an art car as "just another car." How can you look at a car dressed in marbles and think that? Most art car makers do what they do for fun and to be different. One man had living grass growing all over his car. That's different!

Some people don't really know why they make art cars. Tim McNally, who has worked more than three hundred hours on his Plaidmobile, began painting his car after he got a letter from a friend telling him about her new car and how much she liked its special blue color. Tim decided that he wanted a car with a special paint job too. Once he started painting, he couldn't stop.

No matter what you think about art cars, one thing is for sure. If you build one, you will get lots of attention. Art cars are strange, but it's fun to make something no one else has. That is the main reason those who build them love their art cars so much.

1 **What would be another good title for this selection?**
- ○ "The Fruitmobile"
- ○ "Crazy Cars"
- ○ "McNally's Cars"
- ○ "Cars Made of Mirrors"

2 **Most people who own art cars**
- ○ like to grow living things on their cars.
- ○ decorate their cars for fun and to be different.
- ○ enjoy covering their cars with fake fruit.
- ○ decorate their cars to compete for prizes.

GO ON

3 Which of the following is a statement of opinion?

- ○ There are art car parades in many cities now.
- ○ McNally worked for more than three hundred hours on his car.
- ○ It's fun to make something no one else has.
- ○ The oldest art car parade is in Houston, Texas.

4 What can you say about people who build art cars?

- ○ All of them are rich.
- ○ They are all good drivers.
- ○ None of them is a skilled painter.
- ○ Most of them are creative.

5 Most art cars

- ○ are covered with fake fur.
- ○ look like a lot of other cars.
- ○ are unlike any other car.
- ○ have special paint jobs.

6 Which of the following is true?

- ○ All art cars are painted bright colors.
- ○ Art cars are never painted bright colors.
- ○ Some art cars are painted bright colors.
- ○ All art cars are painted the same color.

7 Paragraph five is mainly about

- ○ a letter.
- ○ McNally's friend.
- ○ a new blue car.
- ○ McNally's Plaidmobile.

8 What is the most likely reason the author begins this selection by asking a question?

○ to get the reader's attention

○ to teach the reader a lesson

○ to get information from the reader

○ to convince the reader to build an art car

9 Which detail best supports the idea that art cars have become more popular?

○ It takes a long time to build an art car.

○ The first art car parade was held in 1986.

○ Houston's art car parade has grown over the years.

○ The Fruitmobile is covered with all types of fake fruit.

Directions

Write your answer to Question A on the lines below. Base your answer on the selection "Art Cars."

A Think about the selection you have just read. If you met some art car owners, what would you expect them to be like?

_____

_____

_____

_____

_____

_____

_____

_____

_____

Making Paper

Many people enjoy writing. Some writers are happy to write on any kind of paper. They might use a notebook, they might write on loose pages, or they might just jot down ideas on a napkin! However, some writers are quite choosy about the paper they use, and some even make their own paper.

Making your own paper can be a fun art project. To make paper with many colors, tear up different colored sheets of construction paper. Dried flowers are a nice addition, as are pieces of tin foil. After tearing the colored paper into tiny pieces, mix everything together. Then put it all into a blender filled with warm water. The blender chops up the paper, flowers, and foil and turns them into a mixture called pulp.

After making pulp, pour it into a large pan. Get an old screen, like a window screen. Cut it to the size and shape you want your paper to be, and then slide the screen into the pan. When you lift up the screen, it will be covered with pulp.

Let all the water drip off of the screen as you hold it over the pan. Place a cloth on the surface on which you are working. Then turn the screen over,

GO ON

placing it on the cloth. Use a paper towel to soak up the extra water. The pulp will slowly turn into a sheet of homemade paper.

You will have to do this again and again, depending on the number of pages you want. While the pages are drying, you might want to apply color dyes to them. The dye is absorbed, or soaked up, by the page, turning parts of the page different colors. This makes the pages beautiful. The pages will not be ready, however, until they are completely dry. You might need to wait a full day to allow them to dry.

If you would like to make a book with your new pages, you should ask your parent or a teacher to help you sew the pages together. It is difficult using a needle and thread to make a book, but the book will last a long time if it is constructed, or put together, this way.

After you finish, you can be proud that you are an artist. Now you can fill your homemade pages with your writing!

10 **Why do you need to use a blender to make paper?**

○   to get the paper and flowers to dry

○   to add color to the pages

○   to turn the paper and flowers into pulp

○   to keep the paper from tearing

11 **Adding water to the blender causes the construction paper to**

○   turn white.

○   soften.

○   sparkle.

○   get larger.

12 **After making the pulp, which step comes next?**

○   Soak up the extra water.

○   Add silver sprinkles.

○   Mix in dried flowers.

○   Get the screen ready.

13 **Which of the following is a statement of opinion?**

○ Dried flowers are a nice addition, as are pieces of tin foil.

○ The blender chops up the paper, flowers, and foil, and turns them into pulp.

○ When you lift up the screen, it will be covered with pulp.

○ While the pages are drying, you might want to apply color dyes to them.

14 **What happens right after tearing the paper into tiny pieces?**

○ The paper is turned different colors with dye.

○ The pages are sewn together.

○ The paper is put into a blender filled with warm water.

○ The screen is turned over.

15 **Which of the following generalizations is true?**

○ All writers use the same kind of paper.

○ Some writers like to make their own paper.

○ Writers never make their own paper.

○ All writers like to make their own paper.

16 **Which of the following is a statement of opinion?**

○ Dye makes the pages beautiful.

○ Dried flowers can be added to the pulp.

○ There are several different steps when making paper.

○ Sewing pages together makes a book last longer.

17 **You can tell from this selection that**

○ only adults can make paper.

○ there are not many people who enjoy art projects.

○ making paper is a quick and easy thing to do.

○ there are many materials to gather before making paper.

18 **What would be the best way to prove that the statements in this selection are true?**

○ Read a book about writers who make their own paper.

○ Ask your friends what they think about making paper.

○ Make paper by using the steps described.

○ Look up the word *paper* in a dictionary.

GO ON

Directions

Write your answer to Question B on the lines below. Base your answer on the two selections you have read.

B **WRITING ACROSS TEXTS**

Think about "Art Cars" and "Making Paper." Explain how people who make paper and people who create art cars are alike.

_____

_____

_____

_____

_____

_____

_____

_____

_____

_____

PART 2: VOCABULARY

Directions
Fill in the circle beside your answer choice for Numbers 19 through 24.

19 <u>Imagine</u> a car with mirrors glued to every surface.

What does the word <u>imagine</u> mean?

○ picture

○ listen to

○ drive

○ look at

20 An art car is a regular car that is <u>turned</u> into a work of art by its owner.

What does the word <u>turned</u> mean in the sentence above?

○ twisted

○ changed

○ folded

○ pointed

21 Which word from the selections is a compound word?

○ different

○ hardly

○ grasshopper

○ together

22 One man had <u>living</u> grass growing all over his car.

Which choice is closest to the word <u>living</u>?

○ real

○ painted

○ fake

○ old

GO ON

23   **Get an old screen, like a window screen.**

What does the word **screen** mean in the sentence above?

○   a part of a computer

○   to give shelter

○   a wire frame

○   to hide from view

24   **Tear up different colored sheets of construction paper.**

What does the word **sheets** mean in the sentence above?

○   pieces of paper

○   broad, flat surfaces

○   broad, thin pieces of anything

○   large pieces of cloth used to sleep on

PART 3: PHONICS

*D*irections
Fill in the circle beside your answer choice for Numbers 25 through 34.

25 **Rosa had a <u>loaf</u> of bread.**

If she had one more **loaf**, she would have two

- ○ loafs.
- ○ loavs.
- ○ loaves.
- ○ loves.

26 **One art car has mirrors glued to every <u>surface</u>.**

What word has the same sound as the **ur** in **surface**?

- ○ fern
- ○ board
- ○ hardly
- ○ tune

27 **What is the meaning of <u>prepaid</u>?**

- ○ paid more
- ○ paid after
- ○ not paid
- ○ already paid

28 **With the help of a <u>teacher</u>, you can sew the pages together.**

What is the meaning of **teacher**?

- ○ one who teaches
- ○ not teach
- ○ teach again
- ○ teach less

29   Tim McNally has worked more than three <u>hundred</u> hours on his car.

How is the word **hundred** correctly divided into syllables?

○   hu / ndred

○   hundr / ed

○   hun / dred

○   hund / red

30   Which word is the plural form of the word <u>life</u>?

○   lift

○   lifes

○   lifies

○   lives

31   Tim's friend told him about <u>her</u> car.

Which word has the same sound as the **er** in **her**?

○   bird

○   reason

○   parade

○   large

32   People will try to <u>outdo</u> each other with their art cars.

What is the meaning of **outdo**?

○   do the same as

○   do more than

○   do worse than

○   do less than

33 Which of the following is the base word of <u>artist</u>?

○ ist

○ tis

○ are

○ art

34 **The pages will not be ready until they are <u>completely</u> dry.**

How is the word **completely** correctly divided into syllables?

○ comp / lete / ly

○ com / ple/te / ly

○ com / plete / ly

○ comp / letel / y

PART 4: WRITING CONVENTIONS

Directions
Fill in the circle beside your answer choice for Numbers 35 through 40.

For Numbers 35 through 38, choose the word that correctly completes the sentence.

35 My brothers and sisters are funny. _____ make me laugh.
- ○ He
- ○ They
- ○ Them
- ○ Us

36 Joe helped _____.
- ○ me
- ○ I
- ○ she
- ○ they

37 Sarah has a new bike. _____ new bike is red.
- ○ Hers
- ○ She
- ○ Her
- ○ His

38 I like Matt. _____ a nice boy.
- ○ His
- ○ He'll
- ○ Him
- ○ He's

39 Which sentence is written correctly?

○ I and Eric went to the library.

○ Eric and me went to the library.

○ Eric and I went to the library.

○ Me and Eric went to the library.

40 Which word in the following sentence is a preposition?

My uncle walked to the park.

○ uncle

○ walked

○ to

○ park

PART 5: WRITING

PROMPT

Both "Art Cars" and "Making Paper" describe making something special. Think of a time when you made something special. Write a story to tell about that time.

CHECKLIST FOR WRITERS

_____ Did I think about a time I made something special?

_____ Did I take notes about what I made and why it was special?

_____ Did I tell my story in the order in which it happened?

_____ Did I use words and details that clearly express my ideas?

_____ Do my sentences make sense?

_____ Did I check my sentences for proper grammar and punctuation?

_____ Did I check my spelling?

_____ Did I make sure my paper is the way I want readers to read it?

NAME _____ DATE _____

Scott Foresman
Benchmark Test
Unit 5
Cultures

Glenview, Illinois
Boston, Massachusetts
Chandler, Arizona
Upper Saddle River, New Jersey

ISBN-13: 978-0-328-53741-9
ISBN-10:   0-328-53741-1

1 2 3 4 5 6 7 8 9 10 V016 19 18 17 16 15 14 13 12 11 10
CC1

ISBN-13: 978-0-328-53741-9
ISBN-10:   0-328-53741-1

EAN

9 780328 537419

90000>

PART 1: COMPREHENSION

Directions

Looking through old photographs can be fun and interesting. Read this selection about a boy looking at old photographs. Then do Numbers 1 through 9.

Old Photographs

I never met my great-grandfather. But ever since I found a box of photo postcards he left behind, I have been curious about him.

These postcards aren't the colorful ones you find in tourist shops. They are a kind of brown color, and they are real photographs created in postcard size. Because my great-grandfather was a photographer, I'm sure he made some of them himself. They must have meant a lot to him too, since he kept them in an album the size of a big book. The album has a gold clasp and a velvet cover.

These pictures are from his childhood. There is one set of pictures from the state fair. One postcard shows my great-grandfather and his prize-winning calf. Another shows his oldest sister sitting on a pony. Another picture shows my great-grandfather and his sisters getting onto a Ferris wheel. In every postcard they are smiling. Going to the fair must have been a lot of fun. I live in a city, and I don't even know where my state's fair is held!

There are other pictures of my great-grandfather swimming in a pond with his friends. He is swinging out over the water on a rope in one of the postcards and dumping water on someone's head in another. There are a lot of funny postcards like that.

The best pictures are the ones of my great-grandfather and his family on a trip. In one picture, taken in front of the White House in Washington, D.C., my great-grandfather is wearing a strange white jacket and pants that stop just below his knees. He has on long white socks, white shoes, and a funny little white cap. His mother is wearing a hat with a feather as big as my cat. His father has a cane, a flower pinned to his jacket, a straw hat, and a huge moustache.

In the photographs taken on my family's trips, we're never dressed up. We're always wearing shorts and T-shirts. Sometimes we look like we are having fun, but other times we look hot and tired. Travel must have been more fun for my great-grandfather.

Anyway, I like seeing all these pictures of him. Why? Because once you forget about the clothes and all the rest, he reminds me of me.

1 **What would be another good title for this selection?**
- ○ "Fun at the State Fair"
- ○ "My Great-Grandfather and His Pets"
- ○ "My Great-Grandfather and Me"
- ○ "The Way People Dressed Long Ago"

2 **According to the selection, what is a difference between the postcards in the box and those in tourist shops?**
- ○ their price
- ○ their colors
- ○ their size
- ○ their shape

GO ON

3 **How are the photographs described in the third and fourth paragraphs alike?**

○   They come from the state fair.

○   They were taken on family trips.

○   They show people having fun.

○   They tell about important events.

4 **You can tell from this selection that the narrator's great-grandfather**

○   liked going on trips.

○   was afraid of animals.

○   went to the state fair every year.

○   always dressed up.

5 **How were the great-grandfather's family trips different from the narrator's family trips?**

○   The narrator's family trips took a lot longer.

○   The narrator's family trips cost less money.

○   The great-grandfather's family trips seemed more enjoyable.

○   The great-grandfather's family trips took them to better places.

6 **In the fifth paragraph, why does the narrator compare the feather on the hat to his cat?**

○   to tell readers about his cat

○   to tell the color of the hat

○   to tell what the feather felt like

○   to tell the size of the feather

7   **What does the narrator realize when he looks at the old photos?**

○   that he is like his great-grandfather

○   that he is not as funny as his great-grandfather

○   that he would like to travel more often

○   that he is glad he does not have to dress up

8   **How did the great-grandfather and the narrator look different from each other in family trip pictures?**

○   The great-grandfather looked hot, but the narrator looked tired.

○   The great-grandfather was dressed up, but the narrator was not dressed up.

○   The great-grandfather was always with animals, but the narrator was always alone.

○   The great-grandfather looked unhappy, but the narrator looked as if he is having fun.

9   **Which statement best describes the narrator?**

○   He wants to become a photographer some day.

○   He is curious about his great-grandfather's life.

○   He wishes he had lived in his great-grandfather's day.

○   He likes taking photographs when his family travels.

GO ON

Directions

Write your answer to Question A on the lines below. Base your answer on "Old Photographs."

A   Pretend you are the narrator of "Old Photographs." What are three reasons you enjoyed finding the photo postcards?

_____

_____

_____

_____

_____

_____

_____

_____

Directions

Taking pictures of animals can be difficult, even if you are a photographer and the animal is your pet. Read these tips on how to take good pictures of pets. Then do Numbers 10 through 18.

Pet Photography

Believe it or not, there are some people who photograph pets for a living. Dogs and cats are not always easy to photograph, but professional pet photographers have some tricks they use to help make the job easier.

Pets, like people, have different personalities. So how do you show that? What if you think your poodle looks great dressed up in a pink ballerina tutu? Maybe you think your bulldog will look good with a tiny party hat on his head. How about if you take a picture of your Great Dane sitting in your lap? Pet photographers say there is not just one way to take a good picture of a pet but that it is best if the picture tells a story.

Pets are an important part of many families, and they often show up in family photograph albums. Sometimes they are in pictures with children, but other times they are by themselves holding a favorite toy. It could be a stuffed animal or a ball. What's important is that the toy is one of the pet's favorites. Then, when you see the picture twenty years later, it will bring back special memories.

Pet photographers say that you should not photograph pets from above, but that you should crouch down on the floor so that you are at the animal's eye level. You see things from the pet's point of view if you get down low and up close. If your dog is lying down with his tongue hanging out, even better!

Pet photographers also say that you have to be ready for the pet to move at any time. If the pet you are trying to photograph is being difficult, remember to use food. The promise of a special treat can get the attention of even the most jumpy animal. If you want two animals to cuddle together, rub some food behind the ear of one of them. It's kind of like cheating, but it can help give you a great picture.

The better you know the pets you're photographing, the better your picture is likely to be. First, they're more likely to do what you say, and, second, you know who they are and what they like to do. That helps you take a picture showing their true personality, or charm. Of course, if the pet is yours, then the picture will be even more special to you.

10   **Which of the following is a statement of opinion?**
○   Some people photograph pets for a living.
○   Professional pet photographers use tricks.
○   Pets often show up in family photographs.
○   The best pictures tell a story.

11   **Why do pet photographers sometimes use food?**
○   to get the animal to show its personality
○   to make the animal run and play
○   to get the animal to be still
○   to make the animal smile

12 This selection is mainly about
○ why pets should not be photographed from above.
○ how to take pictures of pets.
○ why families should take pictures of their pets.
○ how to photograph dogs.

13 How will a pet photograph taken from above be different from a picture taken by a pet photographer lying on the floor?
○ It will be sharper and more colorful.
○ It will be from another point of view.
○ It will be funnier and more interesting.
○ It will look better in a frame.

14 What is the main purpose of the second paragraph?
○ to tell the best ways to photograph pets
○ to give some ideas for photographing pets
○ to prove that pet photography is silly
○ to show that pet photography is hard work

15 Which detail best supports the idea that photographers use some tricks to get good pictures of pets?
○ Animals are likely to move whenever they feel like it.
○ It's good to take a picture of a dog lying down with its tongue hanging out.
○ Dogs are more likely to listen to you if they know you and are used to you.
○ If you rub food behind one animal's ear, another animal will cuddle close to it.

GO ON

16 **The last paragraph is mainly about**

○ the importance of knowing the pets you are photographing.

○ the best position to be in to get good pet photographs.

○ the best ways to work with a difficult pet.

○ how some families feel about their pets.

17 **You can conclude that good pet photographers need to be**

○ quiet.

○ young.

○ generous.

○ clever.

18 **What would be another good title for this selection?**

○ "Poodles, Bulldogs, and Great Danes"

○ "Taking Good Pictures of Pets"

○ "Tricks that Make Jobs with Pets Easier"

○ "How to Tell a Story Without Words"

Directions

Write your answer to Question B on the lines below. Base your answer on the two selections you have read.

B Which ideas for taking good pictures in "Pet Photography" could describe the postcards in "Old Photographs"?

WRITING ACROSS TEXTS

_____

_____

_____

_____

_____

_____

_____

_____

PART 2: VOCABULARY

*D*irections
Fill in the circle beside your answer choice for Numbers 19 through 24.

19 **Which of the following is a compound word?**
- O bulldog
- O colorful
- O important
- O children

20 **You should <u>crouch</u> down on the floor so that you are at the animal's eye level.**
What does the word **crouch** mean?
- O fall over
- O stand
- O bend low
- O walk

21 **It could be a stuffed animal or a <u>ball</u>.**
What does the word **ball** mean in the sentence above?
- O a game
- O a round toy
- O a dance
- O a good time

22 **They often show up in family photograph <u>albums</u>.**
Which of the following is a synonym for **albums**?
- O scrapbooks
- O cameras
- O covers
- O pictures

23 **If the pet you are trying to photograph is being <u>difficult</u>, remember to use food.**

What does the word **<u>difficult</u>** mean in the sentence above?

- ○ hungry
- ○ easy
- ○ brave
- ○ disagreeable

24 **One picture was taken in <u>front</u> of the White House.**

Which of the following means the opposite of **<u>front</u>**?

- ○ near
- ○ rear
- ○ lead
- ○ under

PART 3: PHONICS

*D*irections
Fill in the circle beside your answer choice for Numbers 25 through 34.

25 The author was <u>curious</u> about his great-grandfather.

How is the word **curious** correctly divided into syllables?

- ○ cu / rio / us
- ○ cur / ious
- ○ cur / io / us
- ○ cur / i / ous

26 Pet photographers say there is not just <u>one</u> way to make a good picture of a pet.

Which word sounds the same as the word **one**?

- ○ when
- ○ won
- ○ wand
- ○ whine

27 One favorite photo shows a girl, a bat, and a <u>ball</u>.

Which word has the same vowel sound as the **a** in **ball**?

- ○ cat
- ○ album
- ○ pale
- ○ awful

28 Which word has the same vowel sound as the <u>ough</u> in <u>thought</u>?

- ○ caught
- ○ rough
- ○ alone
- ○ enough

29 **What is the base word of <u>announcement</u>?**

   ○ an

   ○ announce

   ○ ounce

   ○ ment

30 **They are a kind of brown color, and they are real photographs created in postcard size.**

Which word from the sentence above is correctly divided into syllables?

   ○ ki / nd

   ○ bro / wn

   ○ cre / at / ed

   ○ po / st / card

31 **<u>There</u> are other pictures of my great-grandfather swimming in a pond.**

Which word sounds the same as the word **there**?

   ○ their

   ○ they

   ○ pair

   ○ dare

32 **Which word has the same vowel sound as the <u>eigh</u> in <u>weight</u>?**

   ○ ceiling

   ○ tight

   ○ game

   ○ receive

GO ON

33 **Which word has the same sound as the <u>augh</u> in <u>taught</u>?**

   ○ stage

   ○ drag

   ○ laugh

   ○ daughter

34 **What is the base word of <u>neighborhood</u>?**

   ○ neighbor

   ○ neigh

   ○ borhood

   ○ hood

PART 4: WRITING CONVENTIONS

Directions
Fill in the circle beside your answer choice for Numbers 35 through 40.

35 What is the adjective in the sentence below?

We watched a funny movie.

- ○ We
- ○ watched
- ○ funny
- ○ movie

36 Which sentence is written correctly?

- ○ The boy told a story about an elephant.
- ○ The boy told an story about a elephant.
- ○ The boy told an story about an elephant.
- ○ The boy told a story about a elephant.

37 Which sentence is written correctly?

- ○ Ray is tall than Nick.
- ○ Ray is taller than Nick.
- ○ Ray is tallest than Nick.
- ○ Ray is more taller than Nick.

38 Which sentence is written correctly?

- ○ Beth is the kinder person in my class.
- ○ Beth is the more kinder person in my class.
- ○ Beth is the kindest person in my class.
- ○ Beth is the most kindest person in my class.

39 **Which sentence is written correctly?**

- ○ My mom can walk faster than my dad.
- ○ My mom can walk fastest than my dad.
- ○ My mom can walk fast than my dad.
- ○ My mom can walk more faster than my dad.

40 **Which sentence is written correctly?**

- ○ We can stay awake go to sleep.
- ○ We can stay awake but go to sleep.
- ○ We can stay awake and go to sleep.
- ○ We can stay awake or go to sleep.

PART 5: WRITING

PROMPT

Your local library is going to throw away many boxes filled with old photographs of your city. Write a persuasive letter to the library explaining why it is important for the library to keep the old photographs.

CHECKLIST FOR WRITERS

_____ Did I think about the value of old photographs?

_____ Did I list reasons for keeping old photographs?

_____ Did I organize my letter in a logical way?

_____ Did I use words and details that clearly express my ideas?

_____ Do my sentences make sense?

_____ Did I check my sentences for proper grammar and punctuation?

_____ Did I check my spelling?

_____ Did I make sure my paper is the way I want readers to read it?

NAME _____ DATE _____

Scott Foresman
Benchmark Test

Unit 6
Freedom

Glenview, Illinois
Boston, Massachusetts
Chandler, Arizona
Upper Saddle River, New Jersey

ISBN-13: 978-0-328-53742-6
ISBN-10:   0-328-53742-X

1 2 3 4 5 6 7 8 9 10 V016 19 18 17 16 15 14 13 12 11 10
CC1

ISBN-13: 978-0-328-53742-6
ISBN-10:   0-328-53742-X

PART 1: COMPREHENSION

*D*irections
Read about a boy who enjoys weather watching. Then do Numbers 1 through 9.

Rain and Sun and Wind and Snow

Tim is fascinated by the weather. He watches the weather reports on television every morning and every night. He loves stories about twisters, hurricanes, and blizzards. He is always thrilled when there is a thunderstorm so he can watch the lightning streak across the sky—from the safety of his bedroom, of course!

Tim also keeps track of the weather in the cities where his two favorite cousins live. His cousin Carl lives in Marquette, Michigan. Tim finds Marquette interesting because it gets so much snow. More than 332 inches of snow fell in Marquette one year! That seems impossible, but it's true. Its annual average snowfall is more than 129 inches. This means that Marquette gets more snow than any other place in the United States except for a small city in California.

Marquette is also one of the coldest cities in the country. Tim knows that even when it's very cold where he lives, it will be much colder in Marquette. It freezes there every winter for long periods of time, which is probably why his cousin spends so many weekends ice-skating and playing hockey.

In the winter, Tim always pictures his cousin walking around wearing a scarf, boots, heavy gloves, and a wool hat. He imagines Carl is so covered with clothes that it's hard to see the boy underneath them.

Tim's other favorite cousin is Iris. She lives near Phoenix, Arizona. The weather there is interesting because it almost never rains. It gets very hot in Phoenix in the summer. If the temperature is eighty degrees in Tim's hometown in Nebraska, it's probably one hundred degrees in Phoenix.

In the summer, Tim always pictures Iris wearing shorts, a tank top, and sandals. He imagines her sipping cool lemonade while sitting next to an air conditioner. He knows that when she plays outside, she has to wear a lot of sunscreen because a kid who doesn't could get a bad sunburn in Phoenix.

Tim also keeps track of the weather in his town. He is helpful to his friends. They know that if they want the forecast for the week ahead, all they have to do is ask Tim. In fact, Tim is planning a bike ride with his friends on Saturday. The forecast said it would warm up to sixty-eight degrees by then, and Tim wants to be ready.

1 **Tim's cousin in Marquette is able to go ice-skating so often because**
- ○ the weather there stays cold for a long time.
- ○ the ice in Marquette never melts.
- ○ Marquette gets so much rain.
- ○ it is usually too cold for the kids to go to school.

2 **What would be another good title for this selection?**
- ○ "Tim Meets a Weather Forecaster"
- ○ "If It's Weather, Tim Loves It"
- ○ "Tim Remembers His Cousins"
- ○ "Tim Starts Learning About the Weather"

GO ON

3 What made Tim think that the weather would be good for biking on Saturday?

- ○ It is almost always warm in his town.
- ○ It almost never rains in his town.
- ○ He saw the weather forecast.
- ○ He asked his friends and cousins.

4 In the fourth paragraph, what made Tim imagine how his cousin Carl was dressed?

- ○ a letter he got from Carl
- ○ some pictures that Carl sent
- ○ a weather program on TV
- ○ his knowledge of weather

5 Tim stays inside when there is a thunderstorm because

- ○ he prefers to learn about the weather from television.
- ○ he does not like the loud sounds.
- ○ he would not feel safe outside.
- ○ he enjoys spending time in his room.

6 Which of the following would Tim probably find the most interesting?

- ○ a tornado
- ○ a warm, sunny day
- ○ a gentle rain
- ○ a snowfall

7 Which word applies to the weather in both Marquette and Phoenix?
- ○ mild
- ○ harsh
- ○ windy
- ○ wet

8 What weather facts about Phoenix interest Tim?
- ○ heat and long days
- ○ record temperatures and high winds
- ○ heat and lack of rain
- ○ sunshine and lack of snow

9 From the selection, what can you conclude about Tim?
- ○ He learned all about the weather from his parents.
- ○ He would like to move to Marquette.
- ○ He spends a lot of time learning about the weather.
- ○ He enjoys warm weather better than cold.

Directions

Write your answer to Question A on the lines below. Base your answer on "Rain and Sun and Wind and Snow."

A Think about Tim and his cousins and how weather affects what they wear and what they do. Compare how weather affects Tim and his cousins to the way weather affects your life.

_____

_____

_____

_____

_____

_____

_____

_____

Directions

Read this selection about a boy who finds a hurt rabbit. Then do Numbers 10 through 18.

Hopping to Freedom

It was almost dark, and Luke was playing in his backyard. He saw something move near the edge of the yard where the grass grew higher. He leaned down and saw a baby rabbit huddled in the grass. Luke looked all around but didn't see its mother anywhere. Luke knew a lot about animals and nature, so he knew the rabbit's actions were unusual. If the animal had been all right, it would have fled by now. He hurried into the house to get his mother.

After Luke showed the rabbit to his mother, the two of them rushed next door to see Mrs. Hurley. She rehabilitated wild animals that had been hurt and cared for them so that they got better. Surely she would know how to take care of the rabbit.

Mrs. Hurley went to Luke's yard to look at the rabbit. She gently scooped the rabbit up in her hands, and held it close to her body. Then they all went back to Mrs. Hurley's house. There she examined the little animal. She said that a dog had probably caught and nipped it before it was able to escape. "I don't think its injury is serious," she told Luke. "But I'll keep it for a while to make sure it's going to heal." Luke watched Mrs. Hurley put the rabbit in a small cage and give it some water.

GO ON

The next morning, Luke visited his neighbor. He was relieved to see that the rabbit was getting stronger. When he asked Mrs. Hurley if he could keep the rabbit as a pet, his neighbor patiently explained why that was not a good idea. "Wild animals have special needs that can be met only if they're allowed to be free. The rabbit will be happier and healthier in its natural home." Luke was a little disappointed, but he knew Mrs. Hurley was right. After thinking about it a minute, Luke said, "Could you teach me more about animals and their habitats?" Mrs. Hurley smiled and replied, "Any time!"

That evening, Mrs. Hurley called to invite Luke to come over. "There is a special event I want you to be a part of," she said. Very curious, Luke hurried to Mrs. Hurley's house.

Mrs. Hurley led Luke to the cage. She said, "It's time to release the rabbit." Luke picked up the animal, and then he and Mrs. Hurley walked to her backyard. Luke looked at the woods at the edge of the yard.

When Mrs. Hurley nodded to Luke, he crouched down. Then he placed his hands on the grass, allowing the rabbit to go free. It hopped a few times before turning and looking back at Luke. He raised his hand to wave, and the animal was gone in a flash.

"That rabbit is happy right now," said Luke.

"Freedom is a happy thing," said Mrs. Hurley.

10   What happened first in the story?
- ○   Luke asked if he could keep a rabbit.
- ○   Mrs. Hurley put a rabbit in a cage.
- ○   Luke found a baby rabbit.
- ○   Mrs. Hurley examined a rabbit.

11   This story is mostly about
- ○   a boy who finds an animal but cannot keep it.
- ○   a neighbor who will not let a boy hurt an animal.
- ○   a boy who knows how to help hurt animals.
- ○   a neighbor who helps hurt animals get better.

12   What was the main problem in the story?
- ○   Luke wanted to keep the rabbit.
- ○   A baby rabbit was hurt.
- ○   Mrs. Hurley worked with hurt animals.
- ○   A dog was running through the neighborhood.

13 What happened when Luke asked if he could keep the rabbit?

○ Mrs. Hurley became angry and told Luke no.

○ Mrs. Hurley gave Luke the rabbit and the cage.

○ Mrs. Hurley set the rabbit free in her backyard.

○ Mrs. Hurley told Luke why he could not keep the rabbit.

14 How was the problem in the story solved?

○ The rabbit was put in a cage and watched.

○ The rabbit was given to Luke as a pet.

○ The rabbit was cared for and then set free.

○ The rabbit hopped into the woods.

15 Which word best describes Luke?

○ kind

○ scared

○ curious

○ patient

16 What is the big idea in the story?

○ Children do not like to be disappointed.

○ All living things need to be free.

○ You have to be patient to help animals.

○ Nature can sometimes be cruel.

GO ON

17 You can conclude that people who help injured animals are

  ○ active.

  ○ confused.

  ○ fearless.

  ○ caring.

18 Luke knew the rabbit was hurt when he found it because

  ○ its mother was not nearby.

  ○ Mrs. Hurley told him.

  ○ it was hiding in tall grass.

  ○ it did not run away.

Directions

Write your answer to Question B on the lines below. Base your answer on the two selections you have read.

B Think about Tim from "Rain and Sun and Wind and Snow" and Luke from "Hopping to Freedom." Tell what Tim and Luke might talk about if they met.

WRITING ACROSS TEXTS

_____

_____

_____

_____

_____

_____

_____

_____

_____

PART 2: VOCABULARY

*D*irections
Fill in the circle beside your answer choice for Numbers 19 through 24.

19 The boy in the story is always <u>thrilled</u> when there is a thunderstorm.

Which of the following words means the opposite of **thrilled**?

- ○ afraid
- ○ bored
- ○ surprised
- ○ interested

20 Luke knew the rabbit's actions were <u>unusual</u> because, if the animal had been all right, it would have fled by now.

Which of the following words means the same as **unusual**?

- ○ twice as usual
- ○ extremely usual
- ○ not usual
- ○ more usual

21 Tim finds Marquette <u>interesting</u> because it gets so much snow.

Which of the following words means the opposite of **interesting**?

- ○ dull
- ○ cold
- ○ fun
- ○ different

22 Since Mrs. Hurley <u>rehabilitated</u> wild animals that had been hurt, she would know how to help the rabbit.

What is the meaning of **rehabilitated**?

- ○ collected
- ○ calmed down
- ○ looked for
- ○ healed

23 Tim is <u>helpful</u> to his friends.

The word **helpful** means

- ○ helps again.
- ○ does not help.
- ○ full of help.
- ○ helps too much.

24 **Which of these words contains a prefix?**

- ○ nobody
- ○ dislike
- ○ special
- ○ blowing

PART 3: PHONICS

Directions

Fill in the circle beside your answer choice for Numbers 25 through 34.

25 He imagines her sipping <u>cool</u> lemonade while sitting next to an air conditioner.

Which word has the same sound as the **oo** in **cool**?

- ○ took
- ○ clue
- ○ trunk
- ○ could

26 Luke knew the rabbit's <u>actions</u> were unusual.

Which word has the same sound as the **tion** in **actions**?

- ○ special
- ○ reason
- ○ expression
- ○ shown

27 Tim pictures his cousin walking <u>around</u> wearing a scarf, boots, gloves, and a wool hat.

Which of the following words has the same beginning sound as **around**?

- ○ age
- ○ action
- ○ aim
- ○ above

28 In which word do the letters <u>im</u> mean "not"?

- ○ imagine
- ○ impossible
- ○ limping
- ○ improve

29   Which of the following words has the same sound as the <u>oo</u> in <u>shook</u>?

○   cold

○   food

○   blow

○   push

30   Mrs. Hurley said the rabbit needed to be in its <u>natural</u> home.

Which word is related to **<u>natural</u>**?

○   name

○   nature

○   navy

○   national

31   Which word means "not costing much money"?

○   inexpensive

○   unworthy

○   extravagant

○   improbable

32   Which of the following words is broken into syllables correctly?

○   disre / spect

○   unc / rowd / ed

○   re / play / ing

○   war / mest

33 **Tim lived in Nebraska.**

Which word has the same ending sound as **Nebraska**?

- ○ banana
- ○ today
- ○ really
- ○ paw

34 **Luke's neighbor patiently explained why that was not a good idea.**

Which word is related to **patiently**?

- ○ partly
- ○ important
- ○ impatience
- ○ patterns

PART 4: WRITING CONVENTIONS

Directions
Fill in the circle beside your answer choice for Numbers 35 through 40.

35 **Which sentence is written correctly?**
- ○ I was in Texas in July and august.
- ○ I was in Texas in July and August.
- ○ I was in Texas in july and august.
- ○ I was in Texas in JULY and AUGUST.

36 **Which sentence is written correctly?**
- ○ My teacher is Mr. Jones.
- ○ My teacher is Mr Jones.
- ○ My teacher is M.r. Jones.
- ○ My teacher is mr. Jones.

37 **What is the best way to combine these two sentences?**

Tim cleans his room on Saturdays. Tim plays soccer on Saturdays.
- ○ Tim cleans his room but plays soccer on Saturdays.
- ○ Tim he cleans his room on Saturdays and Tim plays soccer.
- ○ Tim cleans his room and plays soccer on Saturdays.
- ○ Cleaning his room and playing soccer Tim on Saturdays.

38 **Which sentence is written correctly?**
- ○ Tim tracks the weather in Marquette, Phoenix, and his hometown in Nebraska.
- ○ Tim tracks the weather in Marquette Phoenix, and his hometown in Nebraska.
- ○ Tim tracks the weather in Marquette Phoenix and his hometown, in Nebraska.
- ○ Tim tracks the weather in Marquette, Phoenix and, his hometown in Nebraska.

39 **Which sentence is written correctly?**

○ Tim says, "Iris and Carl are my cousins."

○ "Tim says, Iris and Carl are my cousins."

○ Tim says, "Iris and Carl are my cousins.

○ Tim says "Iris and Carl are my cousins."

40 **What is the best way to combine these two sentences?**

Jan likes to read. Roy likes to read.

○ Jan likes Roy to read.

○ Jan likes as well as Roy likes to read.

○ Jan likes and Roy likes to read.

○ Jan and Roy like to read.

PART 5: WRITING

PROMPT

"Hopping to Freedom" tells about Luke's experience with an animal. Think of an experience you had with an animal. Describe what happened. Give as many details as possible.

CHECKLIST FOR WRITERS

_____ Did I think about an experience I had with an animal?

_____ Did I provide enough details in my writing to "paint" a picture of the event?

_____ Did I organize my description in a logical way?

_____ Do my sentences make sense?

_____ Did I check my sentences for proper grammar and punctuation?

_____ Did I check my spelling?

_____ Did I make sure my paper is the way I want readers to read it?

NAME _____   DATE _____

Scott Foresman
Benchmark Test
End-of-Year

Glenview, Illinois
Boston, Massachusetts
Chandler, Arizona
Upper Saddle River, New Jersey

Reading STREET
Grade 3

ISBN-13: 978-0-328-53743-3
ISBN-10:   0-328-53743-8

ISBN-13: 978-0-328-53743-3
ISBN-10:   0-328-53743-8

1 2 3 4 5 6 7 8 9 10 V016 19 18 17 16 15 14 13 12 11 10
CC1

9 780328 537433
90000>
EAN

PART 1: COMPREHENSION

Directions
Do best friends always have to do everything together? Read the following story. Then do Numbers 1 through 9.

Best Friends Do Everything Together

"Remember that tomorrow afternoon we sign up for baseball," Megan said to Jackie after school.

"Baseball?" Jackie answered in disbelief. "I have zero baseball-playing experience!"

"Come on, Jackie. We're best friends!" Megan argued.

"I understand," Jackie said with a groan. "Best friends do everything together." She sighed. "Ok, Megan. I'll try to become an athlete if we also sign up for chorus together."

"Chorus?" Megan's face looked like she had swallowed a whole lemon. "Music is not my favorite subject!"

Jackie grinned. "Best friends do everything together, right?"

On Tuesday afternoon, Megan and Jackie attended baseball practice. When it was Megan's turn to bat, she slugged the ball all the way past the center fielder. Then Jackie's chance came. She spun all the way around trying to hit the ball, but the only thing she hit was air.

The coach, Mr. Brown, batted some ground balls. He hit the first ball to Megan. She bent quickly, trapped the ball in her glove, and made a perfect throw to first base. The next ball was for Jackie. By the time she got her glove to the ground, the ball had shot past her legs onto the playground next to the ball field. She spent the next two minutes chasing it. At the end of practice, Megan felt wonderful. Jackie just felt exhausted and discouraged.

The school chorus practiced on Wednesday afternoon. Jackie sang beautifully. Several times Ms. Turner, the chorus teacher, asked Jackie to demonstrate how the music should sound. Megan, however, couldn't seem to fit in, no matter how hard she tried. Her voice always sounded too high or too low. When the practice was over, Megan had a headache and was in a very bad mood.

The next morning, Jackie and Megan found each other in the hall before school. "I have something important to tell you," they both said at once. Embarrassed, they began laughing.

"Me first!" Jackie said. "Megan, you're my best friend, but I'm not athletic enough for baseball."

"You're my best friend too," Megan replied, "but I'm not musical enough for chorus."

"I have a brilliant idea!" exclaimed Jackie. "You be the athlete, and I'll be your biggest fan."

"And I'll clap the loudest at your musical events!" Megan smiled, feeling relieved. "Maybe doing everything together isn't important. Maybe the important idea is to support each other in whatever we do."

Jackie replied, "I agree!" And the two friends walked to class.

1 **Which of these best states the theme of this story?**
- ○ Be friends with everyone.
- ○ Work hard today to prepare for tomorrow.
- ○ Music is more important than athletics.
- ○ Good friends can like different things.

GO ON

2 What can you conclude about Megan and Jackie?

○ They wanted to be good students.

○ They were jealous of each other.

○ They both were talented in their own ways.

○ They were often in a bad mood.

3 This selection is mainly about

○ the importance of school activities.

○ how one friend helped another friend.

○ an athletic girl.

○ how friends solved a problem.

4 You can tell that Megan and Jackie

○ cared about their friendship.

○ were selfish.

○ had no other friends.

○ were shy.

5 How did Megan and Jackie solve their problem?

○ Jackie became a baseball player.

○ They agreed to support each other's hobbies.

○ Megan became a member of the chorus.

○ They decided to find other best friends.

6 The author most likely wrote "Best Friends Do Everything Together" to

○ convince readers to try new things.

○ describe how important school activities are.

○ tell an entertaining story about friendship.

○ teach readers how to make new friends.

7 Which of these happened second in the selection?

○ The girls went to baseball practice.

○ Jackie said she had no baseball experience.

○ The girls signed up for baseball.

○ Megan got a headache from practicing music.

8 How were Megan and Jackie different?

○ Megan was calm, and Jackie was nervous.

○ Megan liked music, and Jackie liked baseball.

○ Megan was kind, and Jackie was greedy.

○ Megan was a good athlete, and Jackie was a good singer.

9 In the middle part of the story, Megan felt great because

○ she had learned how to sing in the school chorus.

○ she had agreed to go to baseball practice with Jackie.

○ she had agreed to go to chorus with Jackie.

○ she had done well at baseball practice.

GO ON

Directions

Friendship between two people does not mean that they have to be together all of the time. Read this story about two friends. Then do Numbers 10 through 18.

We Can Still Be Friends

Rachel and Christopher had been next-door neighbors and best friends forever, or at least for as long as they could remember. They also attended Northport Elementary School together. Christopher's mom took them to school, and Rachel's mom picked them up in the afternoons. Rachel was in Mr. Bennett's class, and Christopher was in Ms. Ling's class. But they shared everything that happened during the day on their way home.

Afternoons when the weather was pleasant, they did their homework and then played outside until time for dinner. When the weather was too wet or cold, they stayed inside and quietly played board games on Christopher's game table. Their favorite game was chess. It took a little while to learn, but Christopher's mom helped them, and soon they could play on their own. They took turns playing at each other's house. Sometimes an after-school game would continue for two or three days.

One Saturday afternoon, Rachel's mom said, "We haven't seen Christopher today. That's very unusual, especially since you two haven't finished your chess game yet. I hope he isn't sick."

"I'll find him," Rachel replied and walked out the front door.

She spotted Christopher within seconds, sitting on his front steps, head down, forehead in his hands. "What's wrong?" Rachel asked quietly.

"We're moving to Smithtown, where my grandmother lives," he sighed.

"Oh no!" Rachel exclaimed, shocked. "Where is Smithtown?"

"It's a hundred miles away, so I'll have to go to a different school and make all new friends."

"I'll always be your friend," Rachel said in a comforting voice.

"How?" Christopher asked. "We won't get to play together anymore."

"Let's work together to figure something out."

They sat on the steps, feeling gloomy. Finally Rachel said, "We can still play chess together! Remember when your mom explained how to write down the moves so we could play in the car? We can send letters to each other in the mail. It's slower than playing in person, so it will take some patience. It can still be exciting."

Christopher managed to smile just a little and said, "Ok, Rachel. Thanks."

When moving day arrived, Rachel and Christopher were sad. But Rachel had a secret that made her feel a little happier. There was a letter waiting for Christopher at his new house in Smithtown, and in it was Rachel's first move in their chess game.

Three days later, Rachel received a letter from Christopher. "Here's my first chess move," he wrote. "I'm planning to be the champion this time. My mom said we can visit you during our winter vacation, so I'll see you soon!"

10 **Which of the following shows that Rachel was clever?**

○   She played board games with Christopher.

○   She told Christopher that she would always be his friend.

○   She had the idea to play chess through the mail.

○   She was a good student at Northport Elementary School.

11 **You can conclude that people who play chess through the mail have to be**

○   unusual.

○   friendly.

○   kind.

○   patient.

12 At the end of the story, you can tell that Christopher thought

○ his family would move back to their old neighborhood.

○ he could make new friends and keep his old friends.

○ playing board games was more fun than playing outside.

○ friends had to be together every day to stay friends.

13 What was the problem in this story?

○ Rachel was a better chess player than Christopher.

○ Rachel and Christopher were both feeling sad.

○ Christopher was moving far away from Rachel.

○ Rachel and Christopher were in different classes.

14 If this story needed a new name, which name would be best?

○ "Moving to Smithtown"

○ "A Different Way to Play Chess"

○ "Christopher's Games"

○ "A Different School"

15 Which of the following happened last?

○ Christopher sent Rachel a letter.

○ Rachel and Christopher rode home together.

○ Rachel sent Christopher a letter.

○ Christopher told Rachel that he was moving.

16 Which of the following is a generalization?

○ Christopher moved to the town where his grandmother lived.

○ Rachel and Christopher had not finished their chess game yet.

○ Rachel and Christopher always shared everything about their day.

○ Christopher wrote that he would visit Rachel.

17 **What is the main idea of the beginning of the story?**

○ Christopher and Rachel were in different classes.

○ Rachel and Christopher rode to school together every morning.

○ Christopher and Rachel were best friends who loved to play chess.

○ Rachel and Christopher lived next door to each other.

18 **What is the most likely reason the author included the detail about playing chess in the car?**

○ to explain how Rachel got the idea to play chess by mail

○ to show that Christopher's mom was smart

○ to convince readers that they can play chess anywhere

○ to tell about different board games

Directions

Write your answer to Question A on the lines below. Base your answer on the two selections you have read.

A *WRITING ACROSS TEXTS* Think about the friendships described in "Best Friends Do Everything Together" and "We Can Still Be Friends." How are these two friendships alike? Use details and examples from both selections to support your answer.

_____

_____

_____

_____

_____

_____

_____

_____

_____

_____

Directions

Read this selection to learn some interesting information about the game of chess. Then do Numbers 19 through 27.

Chess

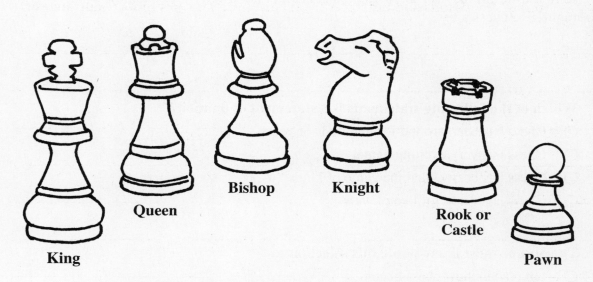

King　　Queen　　Bishop　　Knight　　Rook or Castle　　Pawn

Chess, sometimes called the game of kings, has been around for hundreds of years. Avid chess players get just as excited about their game as do any baseball or football players. Unlike baseball or football, though, chess is played at a table. The chessboard looks just like a checkerboard. It has eight rows, or *ranks*, each with eight squares, sixty-four squares in all. Like checkers, chess is a game for two players. However, checkers is a much simpler game to play.

Each player in a chess game starts with sixteen pieces of six different kinds. The pieces are called *chessmen*. Chess players think of the chessmen as soldiers fighting a war. The smallest pieces, the *pawns*, are like foot soldiers. *Knights* are like soldiers on horseback. A knight in chess can jump over other chessmen, just as a real knight on horseback might jump over a fence. The *queen* is a player's most powerful weapon. She can go all the way across the board in just one move. She can move forward, backward, sideways, or from one corner of the board to another. A player's *king* is not a valuable weapon. It can only move one space at a time. Still, the king is the most important chessman because the object of the game of chess is to capture the opposing king. The game ends when one of the two kings cannot escape.

No one knows for sure where chess began. Some historians think it started in India. As the game moved from one country to another around the world, the way it was played changed bit by bit over the years. Today, a game of

GO ON

chess usually goes on for many moves and may seem to take a very long time. In older forms of chess, however, it took even longer to finish a game. It took longer because the chessmen did not have as much freedom to move about the board, so the king was more difficult to capture.

Good students often make good chess players. Winning at chess takes thinking, planning, patience, and a good understanding of how the chessmen work together. Many books have been written to teach people how to play chess. Other books help experienced chess players play better. Some of these books take the reader step by step through games of the world's chess masters. So if you would like to learn a game that is quiet but can be very exciting, you might give chess a try.

19 **Which of the following statements is a statement of opinion?**

○ Chess has been around for hundreds of years.

○ Chess is a very exciting game.

○ Chess has been called the game of kings.

○ Chess is a game for two players.

20 **The author most likely wrote this selection to**

○ tell readers how chess began.

○ teach readers how to play chess.

○ convince readers that chess is better than football.

○ give readers facts about chess.

21 **The king is not a valuable weapon because**

○ it cannot move very far at one time.

○ it can only move sideways.

○ it cannot move at all.

○ it cannot escape from traps.

22 **Good students often make good chess players because**

○ they probably have read about knights and kings.

○ chess players need to be good thinkers.

○ they know how to play checkers.

○ chess is often taught in schools.

23 Which detail best supports the idea that the king is the most important chessman?

○ Each player has one king.

○ Sometimes a king cannot escape.

○ The queen is a player's most powerful weapon.

○ The object of the game is to capture the opposing king.

24 What is the second paragraph mostly about?

○ why the king is the most important chessman

○ the rules of chess

○ the roles of the different chessmen

○ how knights move

25 After reading this selection, you can conclude that

○ it can take years to become a good chess player.

○ most chess players write books about the game.

○ a game of chess usually goes on for many weeks.

○ most chess players know the history of the game.

26 According to the selection, both chess and checkers

○ began in India a long time ago.

○ are played on a board with sixty-four squares.

○ are simple games.

○ have knights and pawns.

27 Which of the following best describes this selection?

○ It contains only statements of opinion.

○ It contains mostly statements of opinion.

○ It contains only statements of fact.

○ It contains mostly statements of fact.

GO ON

B Think about "We Can Still Be Friends" and "Chess." Why do you think that chess was Rachel and Christopher's favorite game? Use details and examples from the selections to support your answer.

WRITING ACROSS TEXTS

_____

_____

_____

_____

_____

_____

_____

_____

_____

PART 2: VOCABULARY

Directions
Fill in the circle beside your answer choice for Numbers 28 through 36.

28 **Which of these is a compound word?**

- ○ enough
- ○ attended
- ○ everything
- ○ demonstrate

29 **In chess, the queen is a player's most <u>powerful</u> weapon.**

Which of these means the same as **<u>powerful</u>**?

- ○ without power
- ○ more power
- ○ full of power
- ○ less power

30 **"Baseball?" Jackie answered in <u>disbelief</u>.**

What does the word **<u>disbelief</u>** mean?

- ○ toward belief
- ○ without belief
- ○ before belief
- ○ after belief

31 **You want to find the definition of <u>dejected</u> in a dictionary.**

The word would be on the page with the guide words

- ○ degree—delightful.
- ○ defense—dehydrate.
- ○ deliver—demote.
- ○ decree—defend.

GO ON

32 Usually Rachel and Christopher were cheerful. But today they sat on the steps, feeling **gloomy**.

Which word is an antonym of **gloomy**?

- ○ usually
- ○ bored
- ○ tired
- ○ cheerful

33 Christopher wrote that he planned to be the **champion** this time.

Which of these is a synonym for **champion**?

- ○ boss
- ○ teacher
- ○ winner
- ○ friend

34 **Avid** chess players get just as excited about their game as does any baseball player.

What does **avid** mean?

- ○ eager
- ○ unusual
- ○ beginning
- ○ responsible

35 Some books teach people how to play chess. Other books help **experienced** chess players play better.

Which of these is a synonym for **experienced**?

- ○ gentle
- ○ skilled
- ○ foolish
- ○ tired

36 At baseball practice, Megan swung the **bat**.

What does the word **bat** mean in that sentence?

- ○ a flying mammal
- ○ a wink
- ○ a wooden club
- ○ a turn at batting

Benchmark Test   End-of-Year

PART 3: PHONICS

Directions

Fill in the circle beside your answer choice for Numbers 37 through 51.

37 **Choose the word that correctly completes the sentence.**

The coach _____ some ground balls.

- ○ bat
- ○ batd
- ○ bated
- ○ batted

38 **Which of these words is a compound word?**

- ○ practice
- ○ perfect
- ○ headache
- ○ laughing

39 **Jackie said, "Megan, you're my best friend."**

Which of these means the same as **you're**?

- ○ you are
- ○ you were
- ○ your
- ○ you have

40 **Jackie and Megan began laughing.**

What is the base word of **laughing**?

- ○ laugh
- ○ hing
- ○ augh
- ○ laughter

GO ON

41 When the practice was over, Megan was in a bad <u>mood</u>.

Which word has the same sound as the **oo** in **mood**?

- ○ show
- ○ pond
- ○ tune
- ○ cook

42 "Me <u>first</u>!" Jackie said.

Which word has the same sound as the **ir** in **first**?

- ○ born
- ○ heard
- ○ card
- ○ fist

43 Choose the word that correctly completes the sentence.

Rachel had a secret that made her feel _____.

- ○ happyier
- ○ hapier
- ○ happyer
- ○ happier

44 Rachel was Christopher's <u>neighbor</u>.

Which of the following means <u>**more than one neighbor**</u>?

- ○ neighbors
- ○ neighbors'
- ○ neighbor's
- ○ neighbores

45 Rachel's mom hoped that Christopher wasn't <u>sick</u>.

Which word has the same sound as the **ck** in **sick**?

- ○ face
- ○ city
- ○ know
- ○ like

46 Many books have been written to teach people how to <u>play</u> chess.

Which word has the same sound as the **ay** in **play**?

○ straw

○ paid

○ call

○ yard

47 Which of these words is correctly divided into syllables?

○ ma / gnet

○ poe / m

○ pho / to

○ beaut / if / ully

48 The smallest chess pieces are the <u>pawns</u>.

Which word has the same sound as the **aw** in **pawns**?

○ away

○ pail

○ pause

○ town

49 In which word is <u>ist</u> *not* used as a suffix?

○ insist

○ scientist

○ artist

○ tourist

GO ON

50 No one knows for sure where <u>chess</u> began.

Which word has the same sound as the **ch** in **chess**?

- ○ character
- ○ ache
- ○ rich
- ○ shoe

51 "Christopher, what's <u>wrong</u>?" Rachel asked quietly.

Which word has the same sound as the **wr** in **wrong**?

- ○ won
- ○ how
- ○ ring
- ○ when

PART 4: WRITING CONVENTIONS

Directions
Fill in the circle beside your answer choice for Numbers 52 through 60.

52 Which sentence is written correctly?

○ "I like to read books" said Lisa.

○ "I like to read books, said Lisa."

○ "I like to read books," said Lisa.

○ I like to read books, "said Lisa."

53 Last summer Kevin _____ baseball.

○ will play

○ play

○ playing

○ played

54 Which word in the following sentence should begin with a capital letter?

Theresa visits her friend every monday afternoon.

○ visits

○ friend

○ monday

○ afternoon

55 Miguel's mom took Maria and _____ to school every day.

○ I

○ him

○ his

○ he

GO ON

56 Which of these sentences is written correctly?

○ Jennifer's class is having it's big party today.

○ Jacob and Katrina like they're new chess set.

○ Its a hundred miles to Sarah's new house.

○ Shawn and Grace collect coins in their spare time.

57 In the morning Charlotte _____ going to school.

○ has

○ is

○ are

○ am

58 Which of these sentences is written correctly?

○ I drank an glass of milk and ate a egg.

○ I drank a glass of milk and ate a egg.

○ I drank an glass of milk and ate an egg.

○ I drank a glass of milk and ate an egg.

59 Which of these sentences is written correctly?

○ Sam and Jon draws while their sister reads.

○ Sam and Jon draw while their sister read.

○ Sam and Jon draw while their sister reads.

○ Sam and Jon draws while their sister read.

60 Which of these sentences is written correctly?

○ Terry likes apples, but she hates oranges.

○ Terry likes apples but she hates oranges.

○ Terry likes apples, but she hates, oranges.

○ Terry likes apples but, she hates oranges.

Benchmark Test   End-of-Year

PART 5: WRITING

PROMPT

Both "We Can Still Be Friends" and "Chess" are about playing a game. Think of a game that you have learned to play. It might be chess, checkers, or some other game. Write a report that tells how to play this game.

CHECKLIST FOR WRITERS

_____ Did I think about a game that I know how to play?

_____ Did I take notes about how to play this game before I started writing?

_____ Did I tell how to play this game?

_____ Did I tell the steps in order?

_____ Do my sentences make sense?

_____ Did I check my sentences for proper grammar and punctuation?

_____ Did I check my spelling?

_____ Did I make sure my paper is the way I want readers to read it?